THE
POWER
OF
RAPPORT

A practical guide to build trust, increase productivity and develop authentic connections

MIKE GILMOUR

PARTRIDGE

To order additional copies of this book, contact
Toll Free 800 101 2657 (Singapore)
Toll Free 1 800 81 7340 (Malaysia)
orders.singapore@partridgepublishing.com

www.partridgepublishing.com/singapore

CONTENTS

To Maddi and Jack,
May you always know the power of rapport in your lives.
Love dad

INTRODUCTION

"Relationships are the foundation of organisational culture,
and the commitment to build positive connections separates
good organisations from great ones."
Mike Gilmour

As a young boy growing up I found myself often intrigued by human interactions. Whether it was watching my family members, schoolmates or random strangers, I found it fascinating to observe the process as well as the effects of a human interaction. I was intrigued as to why some people were able to connect easily and why it was difficult for others. At this young age I would also find myself evaluating the manner in which I interacted with people and the impact my actions would have on them. I thought this was normal and that most kids were having the same fascination. However, I was wrong. Over time I realised that every human being has a passion, sometimes quite a few, and that human interactions was one of mine.

Later on in life this passion would continue and I would find myself almost subconsciously analysing people or organisations based on how they interacted. To be honest, I learnt so much by watching how badly some people interacted with others and also how society can cause a person to form mental and emotional barriers that prevent human connections. This passion for relationships would cause me to be intentional about building rapport in the various organisations I worked in, sometimes without even knowing it. I understood the value of human connections and sought to build rapport with everyone, from board members right through to janitors, and the impact this had on everyone was always positive. It was almost as if I viewed the world through a human interaction lens. I couldn't help observing these interactions and studying how people responded. While this might sound like torture to some, for me it was, and still is, a passion and I love deepening my understanding within this area of life.

My life was not perfect, and by no means was I a perfect child, but in spite of the challenges I discovered that I had a passion and an ability to connect easily with people. In fact, I remember going to the vice principal's office on many occasions during high school for a range of misbehaviours. However, I found that during these occasions I would leave the office with a stronger connection with the administrator than when I had arrived... and also a few less privileges. These experiences helped me to realise that although the diamond might be rough and abrasive on the outside, there is a passion and value within everyone. I was definitely a rough diamond and I am so grateful to the many people who saw value in my life and helped me along the way.

My experience has taught me that regardless of what barriers may appear between people, absolutely every obstacle can be overcome through building rapport. I am more convinced of this now than ever before. As I grew up during the tail end of *Apartheid* in South Africa, I was privileged to see how emotional connections between people can minimise their differences and ideological perspectives and lead to unity. At the heart of rapport, or human connections, is an understanding that we are all equal, and once a person grasps this commonality they have a foundation upon which to build a connection. Without the understanding of equality, rapport can never be authentically achieved.

Throughout my life there have been innumerable times when I have wondered about the impact positive relationships have on a person or a community of people. What is it about relationships that causes a person's emotional state to lift, their level of engagement to increase and their worldview to shift? Why do relationships matter so much? And, why do relationships affect people so deeply?

These are some of the questions I have been asking myself since I was a child. As I dwell on them and immerse myself in the topic of positive relationships, I not only find answers through my own personal experiences, but I also engage in a journey of discovery that, like an onion, has multiple layers to it.

Perhaps you are on a similar journey of discovery to me and you have already identified the importance of relationships in your personal and professional life. Or, perhaps you haven't and are reading this book to learn more about why rapport matters. Either way this book is for you! I believe that deep down every human being has an intrinsic desire, etched into our DNA, to connect with other people. Therefore, as you read this book, consider it a journey of discovery for yourself regardless of your prior knowledge or understanding. There is always more we can discover about relationships and rapport. If nothing else, I hope this book will convince you that there is power in rapport.

So what exactly is rapport, I hear you asking? Simply put, I define rapport as an authentic emotional connection between two people. It is the inner workings of a relationship that, if developed, should yield positive results for all involved. I will expand on this definition in the first two chapters of the book, but it is really all about a deep human connection.

The Power of Rapport has been written to help people understand the importance rapport plays in everyday life. Regardless of the context, I have witnessed the power rapport has to radically increase productivity and engagement within the workplace. And as important as rapport is in the work context, I believe it is equally important in one's personal life. The ability to authentically connect with other people is a skill we are seeing less and less in the world today. I believe with some guidance everyone can develop the skills required to build relevant connections regardless of the context. So, first and foremost, I have written this book because I am passionate about rapport, and I hope you will be too after reading it. Secondly, I created this book to be a practical guide for people wanting to develop their skills in building rapport as I know my experiences can add value to others.

Throughout my life I have been fascinated by how people interact and why some people are able to build positive relationships while others struggle. I have seen first-hand the impact of a positive relationship, as well as the destructive force a negative relationship can have on an individual and organisational culture. I am convinced more than ever that the ability to build authentic human connections is the most important personal and professional quality a person can possess. Not only should rapport be a skill every person understands, it should be a skill which every person intentionally develops.

While I do believe there is a mysterious, intrinsic quality every person possesses in order to relate to others, I also believe that connecting with other humans is a skill that can be developed through intentional action. Throughout this book you will find practical, easy-to-implement exercises to help you gain an awareness of your current ability to build rapport, and steps to help you start making connections. However, for us to be able to regulate our interactions with others in order to build rapport, we first need to gain an awareness of where we stand through a process of reflection. I encourage you to work through the practical exercises found in the later chapters and take time to reflect on your personal journey. There is no final destination or arrival point when speaking about rapport. It is the ongoing journey a person embarks on in being intentional with their daily actions and interactions.

You will notice that I have included professional perspectives throughout this book from people in various contexts and in different parts of the world. These paragraphs are intended to share a different perspective with you, to give you yet another world view on rapport and why, in the contributor's opinion, it matters to them. So no matter what line of work you are in and regardless of your age or nationality, *The Power of Rapport* is for you and I hope that you are inspired as you read it.

CHAPTER ONE

RAPPORT... SO WHAT?

*"The ability to build authentic rapport with people is the
most valuable skill a person can acquire during their life."*
Mike Gilmour

Imagine living in a world without any form of human connection. Imagine you worked in isolation, you lived alone, you travelled alone and you had no form of socialisation. This kind of existence flies in the face of what it intrinsically means to be human, because as humans we are all wired for connection. We are created with a deep internal hunger for human connection and this is evident throughout history. When we lack these authentic human connections we are generally less effective and less content.

If we look back over the ages it is clear there is one pattern consistently displayed throughout history: human connection. Regardless of culture, religion, ethnicity or location, human beings have an intrinsic desire to connect with one another, whether it is acknowledged or not. These human connections can be found in family, relationships, teams, interest groups, and so forth. Authentic human connections lead to many positive attributes in people's lives, while people living in isolation tend to endure more physical and mental illnesses. Being connected as a human being is being true to how we are all wired.

However, in today's corporate work culture, we are losing the ability to authentically connect with one another. We have largely removed emotions so far from the workplace that many jobs have become purely mechanical. People perform their jobs while watching the clock every hour as it creeps towards 5pm without any sense of connection or belonging. Businesses place a higher value on automating processes that reduce the value of human emotions, intuition and decision making. Ultimately, requiring a human being to perform the job of a robot within a silo. Where are the authentic relationships in the workplace? Where is the sense of belonging and connection that can only come when we place value on one another?

Regardless of whether you work in a school, office or factory, your work environment requires authentic human connections in order to be productive. Period. I'm going to share some strategies with you to help you build genuine connections, or rapport, with people around you. The kind of rapport you will build after reading this book will lead you to success both personally and in your work environment. I truly believe that relationships are the foundation of organisational culture. If we fail to dedicate time to building authentic connections with people, every stakeholder in our organisations will end up losing.

The ability to connect with another human being is known as rapport. However, I like to define rapport as a deep emotional connection and understanding between two people. Rapport is more than simply being friendly or saying hi in the hallways. Rapport is about having an emotional understanding and connection that aligns you and the other person's thought processes and emotions. It is a connection that puts you on the same page and opens the door for collaboration, communication and most importantly, deeper understanding!

For some the ability to build rapport comes naturally, while for others it doesn't. However, regardless of a person's natural ability to build rapport or not, it always requires intentional action to develop and anyone can learn, which is why I will share practical strategies I have learnt in order to help you build authentic rapport later in this book.

My Journey

My fascination with human connection over the past three decades has led me to observe study and research many people and organisations. I have observed high-functioning work environments where team members have established authentic rapport, which has led to success. I have also experienced toxic work environments where there was no genuine connection between colleagues, where team members operated within silos without any sense of care for one another.

I have been privileged to work in large and small organisations, both for profit and not-for-profit, and I have identified consistent traits that are required in order to build rapport. I have also been fortunate to serve in leadership capacities in several organisations spanning several continents, and as a leader I am convinced more than ever that a leader's first objective is to build rapport with all employees. There is simply nothing more valuable to a leader than a deep emotional connection and understanding with his or her staff.

Once a leader has established a good level of rapport with his or her staff they become increasingly easier to lead and influence. This is because one of the most important characteristics people look for in a leader is trust. Without trust no one will follow, engage or truly commit to achieve an outcome. If a leader wants to be effective and seen as trustworthy, he or she needs to build a connection through rapport. This should be a leader's first priority, in my opinion. The leaders who commit to building authentic relationships are more often than not the leaders who lead successful organisations and are able to inspire change and innovation.

During my time with these organisations I have studied how employees connect with each other. It is fascinating to observe the dynamics between people when working towards a common objective. Which employee or leader is domineering? Who is emotionally intelligent and what does that look like? Which employees have a good rapport with each other? Why is this team not functioning?

It is so important to ask these questions regularly as it is only when we reflect on our practices that we gain understanding and develop. The energy and atmosphere you feel in an organisation through your intuition or 'gut feel' is often a very accurate analysis of the culture. We must never forget that employees are human beings who carry their emotional baggage, insecurities and life experiences with them to the office every day. All of these 'external' factors influence their contributions at work. Therefore, by building rapport with these employees, leaders are able to transcend menial work conversations and build authentic connections that harness the power of both intellect and emotions. Rapport is about the establishment of a human connection between two people, and when this connection is genuine the positive outcome influences both the work and the personal lives of everyone.

I believe an organisation's culture is defined by the many relationships and daily interactions between colleagues within the organisation — if they are talking to one another, relating to one another and trusting one another. This is the foundation of a great work culture. Obviously other factors contribute to good organisational culture, but one simply cannot lead an effective organisation without dedicating time to build meaningful connections and relationships.

It is very easy to assess the culture of an organisation simply by viewing staff interactions through the lens of human connections. Whenever I walk into an organisation I observe how the leaders interact with their staff, and in particular, I look out for three telltale signs:

1. Body language
2. Facial expressions
3. Communication style

These signs very quickly tell me whether the leader has established rapport with the employees or not. It's not always easy to quantify the observations, but my intuition tells me very quickly if there is a connection or not. I will elaborate further on these three telltale signs later. This same evaluation process doesn't only have to be used to evaluate a leader. It can be used within any human interaction context and will give you a good insight into the human dynamics at work. For example, you might find yourself at a BBQ (*braai* if you're South African) or birthday party with friends and observing these three telltale signs will tell you a lot about how the people are interacting with each other and whether there is any rapport between them.

Actually, while on the topic of BBQ's, it's worth saying that I find these situations absolutely fascinating opportunities to watch human interactions. And I also love a good steak! If your BBQ's are anything like mine, the men are normally gathered around the fire braving the smoke and behaving like true cavemen, while the women are generally congregated in a more comfortable environment, usually inside the house. The unwritten hierarchical roles of the BBQ are in full swing and everyone generally knows where they are 'meant' to be. The person holding the tongs around the fire assumes final authority like the chief of some long-lost tribe. Surrounding the fire with the BBQ chief are the *impi* warriors (*impi* is a Zulu word for an armed group of men ready for battle), or accountants as they're often referred to during the day. Everything around the fire works until an *impi* dares to challenge the cooking authority of the BBQ chief by suggesting that the meat should be turned or extra spices added. If this happens, buckle up, things are about to get interesting.

All jokes aside, what makes these situations so interesting to me is that not only are you observing people interact with each other, but you're also observing each person's perspective on how the food should be cooked. Throw in a few drinks and you've got the best lesson on human interactions that you'll ever find!

Throughout my career I have made a point of observing how my colleagues and leaders have interacted with me and others. The most common trait among those I had a connection with was mutual trust. We only reached this level of trust after working together for some time. With some colleagues, it came fairly quickly. With others it took longer as there were other gaps that needed bridging — different cultures, backgrounds, experiences, beliefs.

One thing that's important to note is that it's easier to build rapport with people who are like you as there are fewer barriers to overcome. It takes time, effort and intent to build rapport with people who are different to you or who may be similar to you externally, but view the world differently internally. Regardless of who we are working with, our approach to building rapport needs to be consistent, and equal value should be placed on every person you interact with.

Rapport within different contexts

As we continue to define rapport, it is important to note that it will look different within different organisations and settings. It will also look different among different cultures around the world and across generations. For example, millennials, those born between the 1980s to early 2000s, generally see rapport and human connections very differently to those born in the baby boomer generation, which includes people born between the 1940s to 1960s. People born in the millennial generation often place a high priority on being connected to their peers, and the way they build rapport mirrors that need for connection. On the other hand, some older generations like the baby boomers, tend to display more pragmatic and independent characteristics, and therefore their human connections tend to embody those qualities. However, it is important to remember that at its core, rapport is all about the authentic emotional connection and understanding between two people. Regardless of the context, this is always the common denominator and will transcend context.

As you develop your ability to build rapport you will learn that rapport needs to be differentiated according to your environment, as the people you work with are all different. It is not a one-size-fits-all approach. The strategies in this book will help you understand your role in building authentic rapport as you reflect on how you currently interact with others. It is then up to you to implement the strategies within your context. At the end of this book you will be guided through an action plan designed to help you implement the strategies you have learnt. I encourage you to begin attempting these strategies while you are reading, but once you have finished the book take time to formulate an action plan and intentionally begin to develop your ability to build rapport.

I want to reiterate that rapport is not simply being friendly. Being friendly and approachable is important and assists with building rapport. However, an authentic human connection goes well beyond that. Being friendly is at the surface of human connection, but authentic rapport dives a lot deeper. Being friendly and approachable is often a by-product of a person's life experiences and perspective. This attribute is highly valuable and will allow you to make connections quicker. However, simply being friendly is not enough on its own as there will be times when you are stressed, angry or upset, and portraying a happy and friendly face will not be authentic.

Some work environments are not considered friendly, but that doesn't mean rapport is not evident or required. For example, imagine you are a driller at AngloGold's Ashanti Mponeng gold mine in South Africa. This gold mine is 3.9km (2.4miles) underground and the rock face temperature is 60 degree celsius (140 F). Do you think this environment suits itself to being friendly and happy all the time? Absolutely not! It is an extremely dangerous working environment that places the miners under huge amounts of stress. However, is rapport between workers necessary for productivity? Absolutely!

Or consider two pilots flying a transcontinental flight. Is an aircraft cockpit conducive to being friendly and engaging in casual conversation? Absolutely not! It is a highly tense environment at times with strict controls and routines. However, is rapport between the two pilots required in order to keep the passengers safe and fly the aircraft to its designated destination? Absolutely!

It is pleasant to work in an environment conducive to friendliness. However, the illustrations above show that rapport is so much more than simply being friendly. Being friendly is nice and people appreciate it, but rapport is a much deeper connection that can be established even within a hostile environment.

Rapport will look different because people are different. As you develop your ability to build rapport you will realise that what works for one person within your organisation may not work for others. Therefore, your approach to building rapport needs to be differentiated according to who you are engaging with. The strategies I share with you in this book are all relevant, but how you implement them will vary.

Changing a Toxic Environment

As a leader within an organisation it is your responsibility to first assess the organisational culture and then drive it in a positive direction through your actions and influence. I will never forget one particular situation during my time as a young leader in an organisation. This situation highlighted for me the toxic culture that had been created by the lack of emphasis placed on relationships. Within the organisation people had become unaccustomed to speaking to one another due to the toxic culture and in one alarming case, two people within the same room would communicate via email instead of speaking face to face. There was a total breakdown of relationships within the organisation, which meant people worked within silos with very little engagement and collaboration. There were many factors that contributed to the negative work culture within this organisation. However, for me the most fundamental issue was that there was no priority placed on human connections. Now don't get me wrong, most people within the organisation were very well meaning, but by simply *not* prioritising relationships and dedicating time to focusing on people first, the organisation had slipped into a negative culture. The outcome of this negative culture was low staff morale, high staff turnover and a fundamental lack of trust at every level of the organisation. Fear permeated the corridors, resulting in employees only looking out for themselves.

This seemed unacceptable to me and our leadership team. Something had to be done. How could we expect people to work alongside each other, collaborate effectively in teams and build rapport with each other when they wouldn't even have face-to-face conversations and only looked out for their own interests? Something had to change. Our leadership team decided to take bold action and place an emphasis on relationships. As a result, we overhauled all of our staff meetings to become times that focused on people connecting with each other. We were relentless in our pursuit of human connections and used every available opportunity to facilitate people connecting with each other. We knew that we had to be intentional with the little time that we had, and that if we could create an environment where people could connect with each other, people's natural instinct for relationships would take over.

Most of these meetings were dedicated to connections within the workplace while others focused on understanding more about each other outside of the work context. We placed a big emphasis on truly knowing people and seeing beyond their title or position. As a leadership team, we understood that if people could form authentic relationships then our teams would be strengthened and our collaboration as an organisation would be stronger. Rapport was missing.

During these collaboration times, we made use of various team-building activities, strength-finder assessments, social events and other engaging activities. Seemingly small changes like playing music as people walked into the room lifted the energy levels and we absolutely kicked the status quo out the door! We needed a radically different approach to move people out of their comfort zone and to form connections. Not everyone liked this approach. Every change has its laggards, but we knew that if we persisted we would build the momentum we needed to shift the organisation.

The main focus for our leadership team during these meetings was to create an environment where our staff could connect with one another. We knew that we couldn't force a connection between people as this would not be authentic or sustainable. But we also knew that people have a natural desire to connect with one another, so we leveraged this understanding. We just had to make sure that the environment we created was conducive to forming relationships. We knew that the more people engaged with one another, the more momentum would be created. And like a flywheel, once you have the initial momentum it becomes easier and easier. We were looking for rapport momentum.

The result of these changes was phenomenal. In roughly three months we noticed a huge improvement in staff morale and engagement. People within the organisation were speaking to each other, laughing and genuinely connecting with one another. We had a staff team who were building rapport with each other, and as the months went by these bonds grew stronger and stronger. Our teams were more effective and people no longer saw themselves working as individuals, but rather in collaborative spaces where help and connection was just a conversation away.

This experience was a huge learning curve and re-emphasised to me the importance of rapport and how it shapes organisational culture. Seeing the impact of our actions among a diverse staff within an international organisation was an amazing experience. For me though, the thing that stood out the most was that all we were required to do was create an environment that encouraged connections. Once the environment was created, people naturally connected with one another.

So far in this chapter we have begun to define rapport and why it is so important for both personal and organisational success. As we continue to move through the book your understanding of the value of human connections and how they directly influence productivity and engagement will deepen. The professional perspectives at the end of each chapter come from leaders in various businesses and industries, and provide further insight into what rapport means within their context. I encourage you to reflect on these perspectives as you work your way through the book.

So before we go any further, let's speak about you for a minute. The very fact that you have chosen to read this book means that you are someone who believes relationships are important. You obviously believe that rapport matters and you're looking for some guidance, or a roadmap, to help you. I am so glad you are reading this book! There is no final destination when it comes to human connections and so wherever you find yourself on this journey simply commit to keep learning. Businesses, schools, industries and every other collaborative work space need people like you! Relationships, and rapport, are the currency of the future and if a person is skilled in this area I know that they will achieve great things. I hope that this book will be an encouragement to you and re-emphasise the importance of rapport.

I honestly believe the future is bright and it is waiting for people like you who believe in positive relationships. So, whether you're a businessperson, teacher, professional, leader, mother, father or entrepreneur, take the skills you learn in this book and apply them to your current understanding of relationships and you will be set for success.

So with the knowledge that rapport is important, and an understanding that the future is bright for those who prioritise relationships, let's continue to dig a little deeper.

The Importance of Emotions

I'm not sure how much you know about emotional intelligence, but the ability to build rapport is directly linked to a person's emotional intelligence (EI). People with a high EI will build rapport quickly and easier than those with low EI. I will deal with this a bit more in the coming chapters, but just to note that emotions have a significant part to play in the modern workplace.

For many years we were told to remove emotion from all decision-making. The fear was that emotions would cloud our judgement and limit our cognitive ability. In my opinion this was very bad advice, as it is our emotions that unlock creativity within our brains. By sidelining our emotions we reduce our brain's ability to think and feel within a current situation. Yes, unregulated emotions can cause inconsistencies in how we deal with situations and lead to a lack of clarity, but regulated emotions are powerful and vital for all leaders and employees as they actually enhance what we do and how we do it.

Regulated emotions are without a doubt one of the most powerful tools we have with which to build rapport. The ability to enter a situation and sense a vibe or energy is crucial to building human connections, as it immediately connects you emotionally with a person. Once you have established an emotional connection you have the foundation of rapport. Remember my definition of rapport: it is the deep emotional connection and understanding between two people. There will always be a place for cognitive understanding in rapport, but at its core, rapport is built around human emotions.

Every human being has the ability to pick up a negative or positive vibe. It is intuitive. However, many people have suppressed their emotions and do not pick up on these small nuances anymore. The good news is that your emotions have never stopped doing their job. It is just time to pause and start to pay attention to your emotions as they arise in different situations. I'll talk a bit more about this later in the book, but in the meantime, let's start to unlock any hidden emotions because without understanding your own emotions, one cannot develop authentic and meaningful rapport with others.

Some people have grown up with a false notion of emotions, which can lead to a reluctance or avoidance of facing them. Generally, men tend to struggle to regulate or express their emotions, and as a result often opt to suppress feelings, rather than embrace them. There can be many factors that influence emotional suppression, but once people have an understanding of how powerful emotions are, they become open to learning how to regulate them and harness their power.

Do you suppress your emotions? You might not even be sure if you do or not. However, make a decision today to learn how to regulate your emotions so that together with your cognitive ability they can be used as a tool to build connections with people.

Professional Perspective
ane McKenzie, Spartanburg, SC, USA

; as a corporate executive, I found nothing more
nal productivity than relationships. Sure, talent
valuable contribution to any company's success.
ιese attributes are never enough to produce and
ιusiness growth.

_..., ...y career I believed bottom-line revenue was the 'True North' for decision-making. I took the approach of letting the numbers guide my actions from market research to sunsetting products (and everything in between). While this approach helped me increase the speed of decision-making I also lost the engagement of the team. Although I expanded my insight for leveraging our current assets I lost the trust of those I needed to act upon it. Even though my intuition for opening new markets proved themselves out with data I ended up building plans that no one owned and created work that people resented.

What I learned from my mistakes is this — people *are* the business. Without rapport between a leader and the team there is no initiative that reaches its full potential. The reason so many organisations struggle today with adapting to the rapid nature of change and fail to capitalise on so many opportunities, is because they still believe, just like I did, that people are a means to business ends.

That's just not true. People *are* the business. Do you want to see people go beyond the limits of their job description and be motivated and inspired to deliver their very best work every day? Do you want more innovation and creativity that translates into new market share? Then, get good at relationships. Start with these three guiding principles and you'll be well on your way to increased productivity and bottom-line results.

1.   People follow a leader they believe is trustworthy

2. People follow a leader who they believe has their best interests in mind
3. People follow a leader who they believe can help them win at their job

W. Shane McKenzie
CEO
Relevant Leadership Solutions
www.leadrelevant.com

W. Shane McKenzie is a John C. Maxwell certified Executive Coach and member of The John Maxwell Team President's Advisory Council. Prior to founding his own leadership development organisation, Relevant Leadership Solutions, he led a start-up organisation to become a multi-million dollar corporation.

CHAPTER TWO

THE ROLE OF RAPPORT IN THE WORKPLACE

"Rapport is the ultimate tool for producing results with other people. No matter what you want in life, if you can develop rapport with the right people, you'll be able to fill their needs, and they'll be able to fill yours." Tony Robbins

Rapport is critically important within a working environment, but it is not limited to the workplace. Your ability to build rapport with people will extend into every area of your life and will enhance all of your human interactions. Every day we interact with people as we go about our lives, affording us the opportunity to build connections and influence others. However, only people who are skilled and intentional about building rapport are able to establish authentic connections. As we have said, for some people building connections with others comes easily, while for others it is less natural. Keep in mind that the strategies you learn in this book are applicable to every area of your life, not only your professional capacity.

With that said, in this chapter we are going to look specifically at what rapport looks like within the work context. This is the environment in which you spend most of your days. Let's face it, your colleagues are not always the people you would ordinarily choose to associate with outside of work. Not that they are bad people, but they might just be different to you, and you wouldn't naturally form connections with them. This fact can often create tension during day-to-day interactions, especially in times of stress and pressure. However, regardless of your opinion of your work colleagues, a connection is required in order to be productive as an organisation, department or team.

The fact that we work with people who may be different to us presents plenty of wonderful opportunities, together with potential struggles. The fact that our colleagues are different to us means that our perspective on issues could be challenged, refined or enhanced because others see the world differently to us. We are exposed to different opinions, ideas and emotions, sometimes quite far removed from our beliefs, on a daily basis. I believe working in an environment where people are diverse is a great opportunity and leads to the development of tolerance and a broader perspective on life and work. Now, while you and your colleagues may be different, there will always be some commonalities between you and it is important that you identify these. Common ground could be found within your personal life experiences or interests, or could be more work-related, like a shared belief in your organisational vision. Identifying commonalities with your colleagues is essential as it is the cornerstone of rapport and often the best starting point to form a connection. If you search deep enough, you will be able to identify certain things in common even in the most polar-opposite colleague.

For example, if you are a school teacher, your fellow teachers may be different to you and will have a diverse range of experiences that may not mirror yours. However, your commonality is that you are there to teach children. That is your shared passion. I have met very few educators who are not passionate about children and the process of education. Those educators who do lose their passion often leave the profession early in order to find their true calling. This is also true for other industries too.

During my time working in education organisations, both national and international, I have learnt that people have a lot more in common than we often think. Of course, there will be familiarity and commonalities easily found in those from the same country, culture or socio-economic bracket as you. However, I have experienced authentic commonalities in colleagues who grew up on the other side of the world. One international school I worked at had about 250 faculty members and within our wider school community over 70 nationalities were represented. That's diverse! Yet, as I was intentional about identifying connections, I found commonalities I had with people from India, USA, New Zealand, China, Europe, Australia, Sri Lanka and many more. It all comes down to taking the time to identify the connections. If you are interested in the other person and genuinely want to develop a connection, then you will be prepared to take time to identify commonalities. Without a genuine interest in the other person, any commonalities you find will simply be superficial.

As you reflect on your workplace, look to identify the differences between you and your colleagues, but then also look to identify the commonalities. This process can take time, but I want to reiterate that identifying connections and commonalities between you and your colleagues is the foundation of rapport. It will allow you to form a deeper connection and will reduce emotional or mental barriers that may be in place.

Identifying things you have in common is an important step in developing rapport because you will often use this as a starting point with that person. For example, if you have children and you know one of your colleagues has children, this is a perfect open door into a conversation with them. Immediately, all resistance drops as you see each other as parents who face similar challenges at home, not just colleagues. Commonalities highlight a shared humanity and remove any barriers that may be in place due to position or responsibility in the workplace.

You could also find a connection in areas like personal interests, sports, vacation activities, future plans, or family. As you intentionally interact with your colleagues, take mental note of their experiences and interests and see where yours align. There will always be common ground.

Workplace Dynamics

There are so many dynamic factors at play in the workplace. It is a melting pot of human ambition, history, ego and suppressed emotion, and it only takes a moment of stress or miscommunication to turn things nasty. Have you experienced this in your own context?

On the surface we try to keep our workplaces warm and friendly places where employees feel a sense of ownership in what they do. Human Resource departments generally work hard to balance the needs of employees and the expectations of the owners or management. Generally, I have found that leaders do want the best for their staff. However, the superficial crust of a workplace can quickly crumble if authentic relationships are not in place forming a strong foundation.

A miscommunicated email or misinterpreted directive can easily turn into a negative spiral when trust is not present. One thing we can all agree on is that there will always be miscommunication within an office or workplace. There will always be unintended messages that are taken in a negative light by some employees or colleagues. This is because employees are human and often make mistakes, and they also bring their personal and emotional baggage to work each day. This, without a doubt, influences how they interact and operate within the work context. However, if rapport is in place between two employees they are much more likely to understand each other before being offended, allowing additional grace to be extended between people that can limit the damage of a miscommunication, a tough decision or a stressful situation.

Rapport allows you to understand someone deeper. It allows you to trust them by virtue of having a connection with them. If a leader has built genuine rapport with his or her staff they are sure to trust him or her more than a leader who simply delivers directives and expects results. This is one reason why I believe it is imperative for leaders to be intentional about leaving their desks and interacting with their staff. There is nothing more important than trust to a leader, and trust is built through rapport.

In my experience, establishing rapport between colleagues completely changes the dynamics in a workplace. It brings human connection into a usually emotionally-suppressed environment, and it validates people's experiences and perspectives, building layer upon layer of trust. The trust established through rapport is not easily broken, for it is authentic and built over time. When there is an absence of trust organisational culture very quickly turns toxic. Without a doubt employees will fully give themselves, their time and their effort to a leader, colleague or company they trust. However, the opposite is equally true. One simply cannot have an effective organisation that sustainably achieves its objectives without rapport between colleagues, as trust is such a critical component for success.

Rapport forces people to see one another as human beings who can add value regardless of their position within the company. It sees people instead of positions, and allows for a greater sense of tolerance and understanding between colleagues. There is nothing worse than working in a negative workplace where people are not connecting. In these negative environments everyone works within their own silo, getting their job done and shuffling it on to the next person, hoping that what they did meets the minimum requirement and that someone might eventually be grateful for what they've done. There is nothing within a negative work environment that makes employees come alive with passion and enthusiasm, which results in mediocrity and ultimately, high staff turnover, as more and more people are looking for *purpose*, not simply a *paycheck*. Employees want to be part of something bigger than themselves, to work in an environment that appreciates them and acknowledges their efforts.

As I mentioned previously, I once worked in an organisation that had a negative culture and one of the red flags that highlighted the severity of the negativity was that we would have people sitting in the same room, from the same department, emailing one another instead of speaking face to face. People could not simply talk to each other when resolving a matter. Our leadership team was brought in to resolve minor issues, which could have been addressed with an open and honest conversation between the people involved. However, there was a systemic lack of rapport within the organisation and even small matters became large issues as people lost perspective and did not see the value in one another. Fear permeated every area of the organisation, and this created an attitude of self-preservation and selfishness among colleagues. I won't elaborate any further on this situation as I have already mentioned how we as a leadership team addressed the issues and changed the culture.

One of the most fundamental responsibilities as a leader is to build a workplace culture that people aspire to be part of. A culture where people's voices are heard, opinions are respected and value is placed on every stakeholder. This can only be built when rapport exists between all of your staff. It starts with the leader and how he or she builds rapport with staff members. The leader in every organisation must set the example for employees to follow. They will follow the leader's actions far more than his or her words. This places a large responsibility on the leader's shoulders and requires intentionality when he or she interacts with staff. Something I learnt as a leader is that every interaction I have is evaluated by the staff, so it is imperative that I am focused on being authentic and building rapport at all times.

Do not settle for negative workplace dynamics. Address issues as and when they arise and swiftly move on to focus on the positive. Whether you're in a leadership position or not, you have influence and you need to use this influence to build positive connections with those around you. The positive results of an organisation with rapport are exponential and can be measured in both productivity as well as a sense of belonging. Your small, daily, positive interactions will lay the foundation for your organisation's success and, like a snowball rolling downhill, will gather momentum one interaction at a time.

Rapport's Impact on Productivity

It is no surprise that an employee who feels engaged and appreciated at work is more productive than an employee who doesn't. Employees who have a good rapport with their colleagues and their leaders will go the extra mile for their company as they have a human connection with the people who work there. There is a shared sense of identity. The directives from their leaders are not simply seen as coming from someone with a title, but rather from a person the employee knows and trusts. The human connection is so important in the workplace and has a direct correlation to increased productivity.

History shows us that employees who have built rapport with their colleagues are more engaged during the work day. In other words, they are actively looking for solutions to problems, they are positive in their interactions and their outlook on their work environment is positive. The majority of human beings want to contribute towards something, and for most of us it is through our daily jobs. However, if there are no authentic relationships in place employees will adopt the bare-minimum approach where they simply clock in and clock out. In these situations there is no emotional connection or sense of achievement when a task or project is completed. They are simply working for a paycheck.

I have been fortunate in my life to have worked in many positions, in many companies, in which I have a passion. In all of these situations I have been intentional about establishing good rapport with my colleagues and it has enhanced my experience and productivity without a doubt. However, I know that this is not the case for many people and therefore should be viewed as a privilege and not a guarantee. Working closely with people in both the corporate and education sectors has allowed me the opportunity to work within my strengths and find regular inspiration to fuel my passion for people and human connections. Hopefully, you find yourself in a similar situation, one where your passion and your daily focus at work are aligned. Unfortunately, many people around the world today find themselves working in positions which provide a salary but little motivation, inspiration or connection.

When employees have an emotional connection to people they work alongside they are more likely to contribute positively to the work experience and less likely to dwell on the negative through gossiping and complaining. Let's be honest, even the best company in the world has its issues. However, the choice to rise above the negativity is largely influenced by a person's level of engagement and sense of connection. Deep down every human being has an intrinsic desire to belong and to connect with others, and when there is rapport in place employees have this essential desire fulfilled.

There is clear evidence that employees who have authentic rapport with their colleagues have a lower absenteeism rate than employees who don't have rapport. This is because when there are human connections people do not dread going to work. Of course, there may be challenges within these workplaces and times of stress, but people have an overarching sense of belonging which supersedes these daily struggles. For them, work is a place of encouragement, support and connection as opposed to a place where one feels isolated and demoralised.

Absenteeism has a detrimental effect on productivity and employee retention regardless of the industry. Establishing a culture of rapport within your organisation is a vital strategy that can reduce employee absenteeism, and I have witnessed this in various contexts during my career. Without fail the colleagues I worked alongside who had the lowest levels of connection and engagement always had the highest absenteeism rate. Conversely, colleagues who were engaged through rapport and human connections had by far the lowest levels of absenteeism. I have witnessed this trend year after year throughout my career. Therefore, take time to build an authentic connection with your colleagues by using the strategies in this book and you will observe them being more engaged in what they do and more willing to contribute and develop. If you are a leader or company owner, knowing this trend should cause you to emphasise the value of rapport and human connections within your organisation. Like the story I shared earlier, your job as a leader is simply to facilitate an environment where relationships can flourish. The intrinsic desire for connection among your employees will take care of the rest.

In addition to reducing absenteeism, building rapport with your colleagues will also increase the longevity employees have with your organisation. People will always remain committed to an organisation or leader who is committed to them, and everyone wants their workplace to be supportive and encouraging. As a leader, it is your responsibility to develop this culture. A high staff turnover is a red flag in any industry, especially industries that interface with customers on a daily basis. For example, if you lead a school and you have a high turnover of teachers you can forget about developing a rigorous academic program. The high turnover will mean that you are constantly restarting with new staff and managing how you consistently implement your curriculum will be a challenge. If you work in the service industry, such as a hotel or restaurant, and you have a high staff turnover you will never build a loyal and committed customer base, because customers look for a connection with staff. Our customers want rapport as much as our staff do. They also want to feel a sense of connection. After all, this is what will keep them coming back. Loyalty is all about trust, and at its core, trust is about relationships.

An employee who feels connected to you and your organisation will generally be absent less, and they will more than likely remain with your organisation for a number of years too. But most importantly, an employee who is emotionally connected is simply more productive day to day. They come to work earlier, wanting to contribute to the organisation. They contribute in ways that often exceed their job descriptions, and they do this with a smile on their faces most of the time. Why? Because they are emotionally connected. Someone in the company has placed value on them by seeing them as a human being first and an employee second. They have a connection with one or more people at their workplace, which makes them feel included, accepted and most importantly, trusted.

So why is rapport important? It not only builds a culture of trust within your organisation, it also directly affects staff productivity by lowering absenteeism rates, increasing employee longevity and creating engaged staff who contribute on a daily basis. Rapport is not an add-on that you try to establish through a staff function once a year or an end-of-year Christmas party. Rapport needs to be an intentional strategy that is adopted by every member of your organisation and is rooted in the understanding that relationships matter.

Uncertainty Reduction Theory

As we continue looking at rapport and unpacking its meaning and value, I want to share a theory with you. I believe that this theory, while disputed at times, plays an important role in the process of building rapport. It is called *The Uncertainty Reduction Theory*. This theory was developed in 1975 by Charles Berger and Richard Calabrese. Essentially the theory says that when interacting, people need information about the other party in order to reduce uncertainty. The theory assumes that there is a high level of uncertainty among people when meeting someone for the first time. Gaining information to reduce uncertainty allows people to predict the other's behaviour, which is instrumental in the forming of a new relationship. According to the theory, there are two main areas of uncertainty people face when meeting someone for the first time:

1.   Cognitive Uncertainty (Beliefs and attitudes)
2.   Behavioural Uncertainty (How a person behaves)

I bring this theory up because I believe that one of the most important things we can do in building rapport with someone is to reduce their uncertainty with us. When you meet someone for the first time they have a level of uncertainty about you and will be looking to reduce this uncertainty and identify connections with you. This is mainly done subconsciously. Therefore, you want to leverage this theory when speaking to someone for the first time and do everything you can to reduce their uncertainty. Think about the way you stand, the tone of your voice, your facial expressions, your hand gestures. All of these outward actions communicate either certainty or uncertainty to the other person. This is the first step in building rapport with someone you have just met. First impressions can, and do, last.

People will only trust you once they have answered many of their internal uncertainties about you. It is more often than not how you *act* rather than what you *say* that will do this. Very little of an initial conversation is remembered by both parties, but the impression you leave on the person, or how you make them feel, will linger. As Maya Angelou famously said, *"I've learned that people will forget what you said, people will forget what you did, but people will never forget how you made them feel."* It all comes down to the emotional connection that you establish from your first interaction. Reducing uncertainty about yourself in the mind of another person is very important for any form of relationship to develop. Sadly, many people are completely oblivious to this fact and are unaware that their actions, tone and mannerisms during an initial interaction can limit future connections. Gaining an awareness of your interactions as you reflect on them through this book will help you to regulate them for your benefit.

Another area that can help reduce uncertainty in a person you have just met is remembering their name. How often have you been introduced to someone only to forget their name immediately after they've introduced themselves to you? The reason many people experience this is because during that initial meeting your brain is working hard to categorise the other person and reduce levels of uncertainty. Your brain is evaluating hundreds of factors which will create an impression of the person in your mind. Remembering the person's name often gets absorbed by your sub-conscious brain, while your conscious brain works on what is deemed more of a priority. During this meeting your brain is assessing everything it sees about the person in front of you in order to form an opinion and identify commonalities or risks.

Knowing and remembering a person's name is incredibly powerful. It demonstrates to that person that you take an interest in their life. It is an amazing feeling to remember someone's name a few years down the line and see the impact it has on them when you speak to them again. The good news is that your brain has more than enough capacity to remember everyone's name, it just requires training. The next time you meet someone for the first time be intentional about remembering their name. I actually say their name three times in my head while looking at them. I find that this simple technique allows my brain to link their name with their face, and this leads to a higher recall rate when seeing the person again in the future. I'll speak a bit more about my strategy to remember names in the coming chapters.

Something that we need to realise is that our words are extremely powerful. I believe that the words we speak have a significant influence on our lives and therefore being aware of what we say is so important. A lot of people who struggle with remembering names say "I'm terrible with names" or "I'm useless when it comes to remembering names". While often used as an excuse, these statements reinforce your brain's behaviour and your lack of ability to recall names. If you say things like this, stop now. Your brain is more than capable of remembering everyone's name but you are disqualifying yourself through your words. Rather speak positively about your abilities by saying statements like "I'm very good at remembering names". Even if you're not currently that good at remembering names, by repeating the positive statement your brain will be activated to remember and recall people's names. I am a big believer in the incredible power of positive thinking and positive statements repeated regularly.

Calling people by their name is an amazing strategy to build rapport as it shows the person that you have an interest in them. It shows you have taken the time to remember their name and this places value on the other person. Remembering a person's name after an initial meeting will also communicate the message that your last interaction was meaningful and this will reduce uncertainty. Remember, everyone you meet will be uncertain about you. You need to ask yourself: What can I do to lower their uncertainty levels quickly so that an authentic connection can be established? The strategies we discuss later in this book will give you practical tips on how you can remember names more effectively and reduce this uncertainty.

The Role of Rapport in Sales

People will always commit to something they have an emotional connection with. That's why establishing an emotional connection is such an important part of the sales process. I realise that not everyone is a salesperson or is actively selling a product every day. However, we all sell ourselves, so it is important to take note of the role rapport plays in the selling process, regardless of what industry you are in or your job description. For example, you may be going for an interview for a position you've always dreamed of. During the process you will essentially sell yourself in that interview. You will be looking to convince the employers of the value you can bring to their organisation. You are the product you want your prospective employers to 'buy'.

How can you use rapport to help you sell yourself? If you are a teacher, you are selling knowledge every day to your students. How do you use rapport in your classroom to have students 'buy' your conceptual product? If you are in the service industry you are selling trust, loyalty and commitment. How can you use rapport to sell your service?

Selling occurs every day of our lives. Sometimes it takes the form of traditional product sales, while other times it has nothing to do with a product or money but is equally transactional. Establishing rapport with your buyer is a sure way to increase your sales conversion. Not only will a buyer be more likely to purchase the product you are selling if you have authentic rapport with them, but they are also more likely to become a repeat buyer or return customer when a connection is in place.

How do you use rapport within the sales process? In the exact same way you would if you were building rapport with your colleagues. Identify connections that you and the buyer have in common and highlight these every time you interact. One should always value the person before the transaction as this will lead to authenticity in the sales process. Customers can quickly identify a salesperson who is pushing for a sale in order to meet their own objectives and targets, and this more often than not results in no sale or a forced sale, which has very little chance of repeat business. As I mentioned earlier, people want to belong and to be connected, and yes, this is true even in a sales relationship. People want a sense of connection where they trust the person who is selling to them. Take a minute to consider three outstanding salespeople you know. They may be in real estate, insurance or a less direct sales position. What is the common trait that you identify in each of them? It's trust, right? They have built a sense of trust, which results in people buying from them.

Without a doubt you will be more successful in selling if you establish rapport with your buyers. Before you even raise the benefits of the product you are selling (it might be yourself), you should be building a connection with the potential buyer. Get to know them, ask questions and don't be in a hurry to close the deal. There is nothing that puts people off a sale more than a salesperson who keeps pushing. Slow down, build a connection and then work on closing your sale with the buyer's needs in mind.

It is worth reiterating that regardless of what industry you are in, everybody is selling something every day. The product you sell may not have a direct monetary value. It may be a task you require someone to do or it may be a new approach that you want your team to adopt. Selling is nothing more than convincing someone to go in the direction you want them to. Use rapport to build a connection with people and reduce uncertainty, which in turn will help you sell whatever it is you are trying to sell. Without rapport you can forget about a buyer trusting you, and this will greatly reduce your sales conversion rate.

Sustainable Success

So far in this chapter we have looked at what rapport looks like within the work environment. We know that rapport leads to increased productivity levels and employee longevity. These are outcomes that no leader would turn down. However, let's look at rapport from a different angle now. Let's ask the question: Can an office be productive without rapport? Surely one can achieve results with firm, dictatorial leadership and without the need to waste time building connections with people? Well, the answer is yes. An organisation can without a doubt achieve short-term success even if rapport is not in place. People will be miserable and will lack buy-in, but they will get the job done mainly out of fear. While this may lead to short-term success, it is a ticking time bomb destined for detonation. The staff will ultimately leave this type of organisation, decreasing employee longevity because every human being has an intrinsic desire to connect with others. Regardless of their salaries, employees will only tolerate discontent for so long before opting to leave or at least begin actively searching for an alternative career or opportunity. If they are not feeling an emotional connection to their colleagues, leaders or workplace, they are headed towards resignation sooner rather than later.

There are many examples of dictators throughout history. Men who have risen to political power through often very violent means. Robert Mugabe, Chairman Mao and Adolf Hitler are three of a very long list of history's most influential dictators (I use the word influential in a negative way). The commonality I identify between just about all of the political dictators in history is that they were able to rule through instilling fear, limiting personal expression and nullifying any opposition. Often, the tool they used to enforce their dictatorship was the military. I don't need to go through some of the horrific atrocities that the political dictators of the world have authorised as I'm sure you are well aware of them. However, like all areas of history, it is important that we all learn from the mistakes of others so we can move forward.

Nowadays CEOs and other workplace dictators do not have access to militaries that can enforce their authority. Well, I certainly hope they don't! However, the traits that we identify in political dictators can also be identified in corporate dictators. Workplace dictators instil fear, limit personal expression and quickly snuff out any perspectives not aligned with theirs. I have experienced that when these three symptoms of a dictatorial leader are experienced within a workplace, human connections and rapport between colleagues disappears. With this said, it's important to note that workplace dictators are not only found at the top of the organisational chart, they can be found at every level of an organisation and are equally detrimental regardless of how much authority they have. Teams, divisions, departments or whole organisations will endure long-term failure under the direction of a dictatorial leader, purely because relationships are not prioritised and intentionally focused on. Relationships simply don't matter to these people.

On the other side of this perspective, dictatorial leaders can be highly effective in getting a job done, but this short-term success will come at a cost. As the African proverb says, *"If you want to go fast, go alone. If you want to go far, go together."* There will always be greater long-term successes when emphasis is placed on building positive connections with people. Deepak Chopra says, *"The fastest way for a business to succeed in the long run is to take care of its employees."* Both of these quotes epitomise where organisations should be placing their focus if they truly want long-term success. Their focus should be on the people within the organisation. Regardless of what business you are in, relationships matter and need to be prioritised. When this area of an organisation is invested in, long-term success will be achieved.

The most effective way to build a high-functioning workforce that is sustainable and long-lasting is to build your organisation upon a foundation of rapport. Take time to build the human connections in your workplace and you will see the absenteeism rate decline, employee longevity increase and daily productivity skyrocket. Build slow, build steady and reap the rewards of a positive work culture. Build too fast without taking time to connect authentically with people and you're headed for trouble.

Professional Perspective
- Bill Palmer, Spartanburg, SC, USA

Unfortunately, most people's perspective on personal encounters is suspicious or even negative without a basis to counter that. That's why good rapport is so necessary, whether on a team or in a workplace.

Hundreds of conversations a day can test a person's view on relationships, value and purpose. This can leave them wondering where they stand on a project or with their colleagues. Good rapport can make the difference in the level of success for a project, goal or organisational mission. Why? Because like it or not, gone are the days where a boss dictates, and employees blindly jump for the sole sake of pleasing and the results are the best they can be. People need relationships they believe in and can trust. When team members have a relationship that has been nurtured along the way with good rapport; when they work in an environment that promotes collaboration and allows for questions; when they believe people around them actually care about their life beyond the task at hand; then, people want to support, want to work hard, be more productive and want to see others around them succeed.

In my 16 years in non-profit work and 15 years of ministry before that, I can say without hesitation that the work put into good relationships on a team built bridges to success as much or more than anything else. Where there is good rapport and relationships with team members, there is trust, buy-in and selflessness...all of which are necessary ingredients to the formula for great results in any endeavor. I've served in leadership roles where there was good rapport and where there wasn't. The latter produced a cancer within the organisation that diminished and even nullified any success. But, the teams I've been on where relationships were the foundation for great work produced a fuel that accelerated our accomplishments and allowed for tremendous success!

Looking back over the years, some of the greatest work was fueled by great relationships. These relationships weren't created overnight. They took time. And, they took following the commandments every Christian is to follow still today: "*Love God with all your heart, mind and soul and love others as yourself!*" As I worked at this (and still need work), the more I could forgive, be more secure in myself (through Christ) and love others. When that happened, I cared more. I was more interested in them than I was before and they knew it. When a leader exemplifies these attributes, I've found that people want to be on his/her team. I communicated better and they interpreted better. The results were trust, teamwork and success. Relationships truly are the foundation for great results on any team!

Bill Palmer
Executive Director
Upwards Sports

CHAPTER THREE

THE ROLE OF EMOTIONAL INTELLIGENCE

"In a very real sense we have two minds, one that thinks and one that feels." Daniel Goleman

In this chapter we will continue our look into the power of rapport, but in particular we will focus on the role of a person's emotions and the impact emotional intelligence plays in forming human connections. As I mentioned earlier, understanding your emotions is a vital step in developing the skills required to build rapport. Quite simply, rapport is founded on emotions.

According to the Rutgers University-based Consortium for Research on Emotional Intelligence in Organisations (CREIO), "Social and personal competencies are vital for a healthy and productive life. Self-awareness, optimism, and empathy can enhance satisfaction and productivity at work and in other aspects of life. The workplace is the ideal setting for the promotion of these competencies in adults because work plays a central role in their lives. Not only do most of us spend the largest portion of our waking time at work, but our identity, self-esteem, and well-being are strongly affected by our work experiences."

"The workplace also is an ideal place for promoting social and emotional competencies because it often is there that people feel their lack most keenly. When people realise that social and emotional abilities hold the key to greater career success, they become eager to develop those abilities. At the same time, as employers recognise that their profit depends on the emotional intelligence of their employees, they become amenable to launching programs that will increase it."

Emotional intelligence (EI) is fast becoming the number one attribute companies are looking for in employees. In the past, emphasis in the hiring process was mainly placed on a person's content knowledge and cognitive skills that relate to their field of work. However, these days companies realise that content knowledge will only take their company so far; more importantly, it is an employee who is emotionally intelligent who will be an asset to a company. Don't get me wrong, having the relevant content knowledge and cognitive ability in order to perform a task is critical for success. However, without high emotional intelligence an employee may struggle to work within a team environment or interface effectively with challenging customers. These days companies are realising more and more that efficiency largely comes down to human connections and teamwork. Being able to work collaboratively is an essential skill in our rapidly-evolving working environments, and having an understanding of one's own emotions and the ability to perceive the emotions of others is critical to building team dynamics.

So what exactly is emotional intelligence (EI), or emotional quotient (EQ), as it is more formally referred to? Emotional intelligence is the ability a person has to regulate their own emotional state and also perceive another person's emotions. A person with high emotional intelligence will have a very consistent emotional state, which will not fluctuate depending on external influences or circumstances. Someone with high EI will be able to perceive another person's emotional state and act accordingly with the appropriate amount of empathy, tact and relevance. Emotional intelligence is a vital skill that can be developed through reflection, understanding and practice.

As I mentioned before, in the past many people were encouraged to remove all emotion from the workplace, especially from decision-making. This was terrible advice, that I sometimes still hear today, as our emotions are one of our most powerful tools for creative thinking. Our emotions unlock our intuition, or gut instinct, and once honed, this is a vital tool to use when making decisions. With that said, I must add that unregulated emotions will cause a lack of clarity in the decision-making process. Unregulated emotions can cause erratic responses, which are not beneficial in either the long or short-term. It is therefore critical that you learn how to regulate your emotions so that they can work *for* you rather than *against* you. Unregulated emotions will cause fluctuations and inconsistencies in how you relate to people, which is counterproductive for building rapport. Consistency in your interactions is important in reducing the uncertainty people may have about you. A person with low emotional intelligence will find it difficult to build sustainable rapport as they lack the fundamental ability to perceive the emotions of others. However, a person who has high emotional intelligence, the ability to regulate their own emotions and perceive the emotions of others, will be able to build rapport that is consistent and authentic.

Being able to perceive other people's emotional states is crucial as it will change the way you interact with them. If you perceive that a person is sad, frustrated or angry you are able to adjust your approach in order to build a connection and find common ground. A person without this ability could use an incorrect approach and potentially create a barrier, or the inability to establish a connection in the future. As you gain control over your emotions you will begin to perceive others' emotions more clearly and this will increase your ability to connect with them. The key to developing your emotional intelligence is awareness, as awareness is the starting point for regulation. It is only once you have an awareness of your own emotions and the ability to regulate them, that you can more effectively perceive the emotions of others.

Emotions play a very important part in building rapport as ultimately a *human* connection is an *emotional* connection. During the rapport-building process people are 'feeling each other out', their brains and emotions are working hard to identify connections and reduce uncertainty. So don't shy away from your emotions. Embrace them in this process, and as you develop your ability to regulate and identify your own emotions you will increase your ability to perceive others' emotional states.

The ability to perceive another person's emotional state is vital in building rapport. Often an encouraging word or simply being there to listen is all it takes to develop a connection. I have learnt that my actions are more powerful than my words and sometimes all it takes is to be quiet and listen. This can be a great connection builder. If you don't have the ability to sense a person's emotions you won't be able to respond to their needs. It is also impossible to build effective rapport without understanding one's own emotions.

A Practical Guide to Regulating Your Emotions

Okay, so enough talking about emotional intelligence, let's do something practical to help you get in touch with your emotions. This is a reflective exercise that will help you identify the emotions you are feeling. For this exercise I would like you to find a comfortable chair to sit in where you can be free from distractions. Closing your eyes will help you focus and get the most out of it. This is a one-minute drill, so don't worry, you won't be stuck here for hours. Here's what I'd like you to do…

Step One:

- Think back to a recent positive emotion you felt, preferably within the last 48 hours. It could be happiness from watching your children play outside or excitement for an upcoming event. Think about how you felt during this event or experience, and try to identify the emotion you felt. Don't rush this process, if it takes you a while to identify an emotion that's okay. Once you've identified an emotion I want you to dwell on it for a minute and immerse yourself in that feeling, then I'd like you to reflect on two questions.

- What does it feel like in your body?

- Where do you feel this emotion in your body? For example, some people say they sometimes feel emotions in their stomach. Think about where you felt this emotion in your body and how it is different to when you're not experiencing that emotion. Remain in this emotional state for a while and get used to what it feels like as you reflect on it. The purpose of this reflection is for you to learn to identify the emotions you are feeling.

Step Two:

Speak out how you feel after identifying this emotion. Vocalising your emotions is an important part of developing an emotional awareness, and it is something I believe we do not do regularly enough. You might experience further joy, peace or continued happiness as you reflect on the past experience. Take some time to verbalise what you are currently feeling. What you are doing through this exercise is learning to identify the emotions you feel and then labelling which emotion it is. By labelling the emotion and connecting it with what you felt in your body you are developing the ability to regulate that emotion. By regularly practicing this brief exercise you will learn how to quickly identify the emotions you feel, and once you are able to identify and label your emotional state you are then more able to regulate the emotions you feel.

How do you feel after completing this exercise? I hope you found it beneficial. I have found this simple exercise, when done consistently, has the ability to raise emotional awareness levels in anyone who implements it. To this day I still set time aside, regardless of how busy my schedule is, to focus on reflecting and labelling my emotions. Emotional intelligence is a journey and not a destination, and so regardless of your emotional awareness level, spend time as often as you can implementing this simple reflection exercise. It is also important to note that this exercise applies to any emotion you feel. While it is empowering to relive the positive emotions we feel, this is equally a very powerful exercise to use to identify and label negative emotions like sadness, frustration or anger. By reflecting on the emotional experience you have been through, identifying where in your body you feel the emotion, and then speaking out your feelings you will be able to label the emotion and gain control of the feelings you experience. The end goal being increased emotional intelligence.

I encourage you to do this exercise daily until you become so good at identifying your emotions that you can do it even in the presence of other people, during a board meeting for example. Obviously you won't speak out your feelings in this context, but you can still speak them out in your head as you reflect on your emotional state. Use previous emotions as an exercise, but ultimately you want to progress this exercise to focus on your *current* emotions and develop the ability to quickly identify your emotions as and when you feel them. Identifying your emotions when you experience them, and then having the ability to regulate how they affect your actions, leads to increased emotional intelligence. This has a direct positive impact on your ability to build rapport and is such an important step in becoming emotionally intelligent. As previously said, you can only begin to perceive another person's emotions once you have developed the ability to regulate your own, and regulation begins with awareness.

Practice Intuition

Intuition is a powerful tool driven by emotions, which needs to be developed and used in all areas of life. Intuition is a powerful component of rapport as there are many things that you need to 'feel' when interacting with others. These intuitive feelings often surpass cognitive reasoning, hence the importance of unlocking intuition in your daily life. Often referred to as your 'gut feeling', intuition is your body's ability to feel or sense a situation by using all of your body's senses, emotions and your subconscious brain. I believe intuition is an incredibly powerful tool, which people are using less and less these days due to an over-reliance on cognitive processes and the limitations we have placed on emotions within the workplace. After a lifetime dedicated to the study of EI, Daniel Goleman concluded that *"an emotional brain responds to an event more quickly than a thinking brain"*. This is an incredibly powerful statement and one which I am believing in more and more these days.

I believe that one of the reasons we do not tap into our intuition is because of the speed at which we are often required to make decisions. Listening to your intuition often takes time, especially if it is not something you are used to doing. One needs to allow time to think and feel during a decision-making process, slowing down and revisiting the context. But let's be honest, in today's world who has the time to slow down? Or is that actually precisely what the problem is? Throughout the world we are being trained in world-class universities to be so efficient and fast at doing our jobs that this could actually be counterproductive when it comes to decision-making. Over the years as I've worked on hearing, feeling and trusting my intuition and allowing it to guide my thought process, I have found that my intuition is very rarely wrong. And those times where it was wrong was probably more linked to me rushing the process and less about my intuition being incorrect. I have trusted my gut in small daily situations when interacting with people, right up to large-scale situations like investing in businesses or purchasing a property. Learning to pause and 'feel' a situation with my intuition has been one of the greatest skills I have ever developed. But like any skill, it requires constant attention and focus in order to develop. The more we utilise our intuition and learn to hear it, the louder it becomes. Like any skill or ability, the more you use it, the more honed it will become.

Intuition is closely linked to emotional intelligence as it is an emotional connection or feeling that will drive your thought process. In the developed world we are very cerebral in our approach to our work and personal lives, and as a result our emotional intelligence as a society has largely decreased. We need to retrain ourselves to connect with our emotions and use them as a powerful tool in our daily lives to build rapport, drive human connections and make better decisions.

One way to develop your ability to be led by your intuition is to ask yourself a simple question whenever you are faced with a decision. Regardless of the size of the decision, ask yourself, "What do I feel about this situation?" and then pause for a moment to listen to your body and get a sense of what your intuition is saying. This brief activity is best done initially with your eyes closed to reduce distractions until you have built up the ability to do it in public without anyone noticing. The more you listen to your intuition and act on what you feel, the more clearly you will feel it in the future.

Intuition, just like emotional intelligence, is vital in the rapport-building process as your intuition will often tell you more about a situation with a colleague than a verbal conversation. Intuition will give you a sense as to where that person is emotionally, what they are feeling, and what your next move should be. Practice listening to your intuition daily and your ability to be led by it will increase.

I will return to the role of intuition again in chapter ten, where we will look at this important aspect within the rapport-building process. However, it is important for you to understand the close connection between intuition and emotional intelligence. Understanding and developing these two powerful components will be what sets you apart from your colleagues.

Five Pillars of Emotional Intelligence

So, getting back to emotional intelligence, I believe there are five pillars that display high emotional intelligence. While there are many other facets to emotional intelligence, these five pillars are clear evidence of high EI. People displaying these five pillars in their daily lives will have a significant advantage when building rapport with others. If a person is unable to genuinely build rapport with others, or they find connecting with others a challenge, I would say they probably have weak EI.

Remember, each of these pillars is a *journey*, not a *destination*. While people might display these traits regularly, just like rapport, each requires intentional action and development to be effective. It's important to note that one never fully arrives at emotional intelligence — it is a journey of discovery for each of us. Complacency in the area of emotional intelligence can be as detrimental as complacency in other areas of your life. So, regardless of how emotionally intelligent you are, there is always more to learn and develop. Reaching a deeper emotional awareness will lead to a greater ability to regulate one's own emotions more effectively.

Three of the five pillars we will discuss relate *externally* to the people around you, while the other two focus *inwardly*. This is intentional, as people who have high emotional intelligence will instinctively place importance on those around them, and this will be evident in their daily interactions. A person with low EI will generally focus attention on their emotional state to the point where they become oblivious to the emotions of those around them. Let's have a look at the five pillars of emotional intelligence.

Pillar One — Emotional Awareness

This is the most important pillar, because without understanding your own emotions it is impossible to perceive the emotions of someone else. Understanding and having the ability to regulate your emotions is critical to developing emotional intelligence. Take time every day to practice the exercises mentioned in this chapter and you will begin to truly feel and control your emotions, and therefore be in a better position to perceive the emotions of others.

Remember that understanding your emotions does not happen overnight. It comes with time and experience. However, the process can be intentionally fast-tracked by taking the time to reflect on your emotions and how they influence your actions. Our emotions are exceptionally powerful attributes that can either work for us or against us, depending on our ability to regulate them. Therefore, it is important, like with any attribute, that you gain awareness of them so that you can control them.

Jack Ma, the founder of Alibaba.com and internet pioneer in China, says that *"Knowledge can be acquired through hard work, but wisdom is acquired through experience"*. I believe that wisdom and emotional intelligence are very closely linked as I am yet to meet a person who I would describe as wise who has low emotional intelligence. So as wisdom comes through experience, so too does emotional awareness. Being aware of your emotions is the first and most important pillar of emotional intelligence. Awareness takes time and develops through experience, but it can be fast-tracked when a person is intentional about developing it.

Pillar Two — Exuding Gratitude

An attitude of gratitude will alter one's perspective on life and dramatically change all human interactions in a positive way. By intentionally identifying things you are grateful for and communicating these to yourself and those around you, your brain immediately switches to a positive, growth mindset. It is amazing how the small, seemingly insignificant action of being grateful can so radically change your perspective and perception of the world and people around you. Gratitude is often the defining characteristic of a positive person, while a lack of gratitude is almost always associated with negative people, or inwardly-focused people. Exuding gratitude in your daily life will set you apart from others and draw people towards you. And as the phrase 'exuding gratitude' suggests, it is the ability to transfer your positive disposition onto others through your demonstrated actions of gratitude.

I believe emotionally intelligent people are intentional about living a life of gratitude, which is then imparted to others, as emotionally intelligent people are more focused on others than on themselves. I hear you asking, so what makes an emotionally intelligent person grateful? Well, firstly I believe that gratitude is a choice that people make every day. However, this choice can only be authentically made by a person who is secure in themselves and their emotions as it is only when one is secure in who they are that they can remove the focus from themself and place it on people around them. Equally important, people who exude gratitude demonstrate a balanced perspective in how they view all aspects of life. This trait is common among emotionally intelligent people.

I believe that exuding gratitude can help us in all contexts of life. When we face a negative situation it can often easily be reframed in our mind into something positive by using the power of gratitude. By choosing to be grateful, regardless of how challenging the situation, we automatically redirect our brain to focus on the positive. Of course, not everything goes according to plan in life. It can be pretty ugly at times. However, I believe the best way to counter a negative experience is to focus on what you're grateful for. An attitude of gratitude reframes our brain's perspective on the world, and frustrations or negativity dissolve as you view circumstances from a larger perspective. Not only is exuding gratitude beneficial for ourselves and building rapport, being grateful for everything you have is contagious and others can identify with the positive disposition you display. Actually, it is a highly attractive quality. Gratitude is infectious. Take time every morning, before checking your messages or emails, to speak out what you are grateful for and watch your perspective on the world change. By speaking out your gratitude you are declaring a positive mindset, and your brain and emotions will respond accordingly. As you exude gratitude you will positively influence those around you without even realising it.

I have experienced firsthand how gratitude can positively influence both colleagues and organisations. Having been fortunate to work in a wide range of organisations on several continents, I have experienced a clear distinction between people who exude gratitude and those who don't. Without a doubt the people who exuded gratitude in their interactions and perspectives were more emotionally intelligent people, they were able to regulate their emotions and perceive the emotional state of others. These experiences reinforce my belief that emotionally intelligent people exude gratitude in their daily lives regardless of challenging circumstances. I distinctly remember one situation while sitting in a leadership meeting of a large organisation that was facing several significant challenges. As we discussed financial statements, staff restructuring and increased competition it was very clear that our outlook was bleak. In that moment as a team we had lost perspective due to what seemed to be insurmountable challenges. Everything looked bad and as a result we were not able to identify solutions. However, in that moment as a leadership team we realised that we had lost perspective and we needed to shift our mindsets into a positive mode. How did we do this? By exuding gratitude! We began to speak out all the positive aspects of the organisation, regardless of how small they were. We chose to speak out our gratitude in the midst of the challenge and as we began focusing on what was going well and vocalising our gratitude the whole atmosphere in the meeting changed. All of a sudden the weak balance sheet and impending staff restructure became opportunities instead of obstacles. Our perspective had changed through intentionally exuding gratitude and the result was a team that became proactive in finding solutions in spite of the challenges. I learnt a lot from that experience as it proved to me the power that is found in exuding gratitude.

You see, it only takes one person exuding gratitude for positivity to spread. Exuding gratitude indicates that a person is not limited by their own emotional state, but they are able to proactively regulate their emotions towards gratitude and then influence those around them. People with low emotional intelligence struggle to consistently exude gratitude as they are heavily influenced by emotional spikes in their own lives. Some days they're up, while others they're down and this lack of consistency and the inability to consistently exude gratitude causes uncertainty among people around them. However, emotionally intelligent people are able to regulate their emotions more effectively during the natural highs and lows of life, which leads to a more consistent appreciation of the world and the people around them.

Pillar Three — Displaying Empathy

Empathy is a powerful emotion. While we all have the ability to be empathetic of another person's situation, it is only when that empathy transitions into meaningful action that it becomes a powerful tool for rapport. At its very core, empathy is simply placing yourself in another person's position and understanding things from their perspective.

One cannot be empathetic yet disengaged, as empathy is a very active, expressive emotion that requires human interaction.

When emotionally intelligent people interact with others, they constantly consider the other person's emotional state and well-being. By intentionally placing yourself in a position where you can truly understand another person's perspective you are demonstrating emotional intelligence. Only then can you act in a way that is authentic and supportive. I believe empathy is a rapidly diminishing emotion in today's fast-paced world, yet the world craves it. Emotionally intelligent people disrupt the status quo by actively displaying empathy during their daily interactions with others. Think about people you interact with on a regular basis. Would you define the people who regularly display empathy as emotionally intelligent? I have not met many people who genuinely display empathy for others who don't meet my general definition of high emotional intelligence. For me, displaying empathy is an attribute of emotional intelligence. Hence it's a pillar!

Pillar Four — Authentic Praise

One of the most effective ways to build rapport with someone is to build them up emotionally. In other words, make them feel good about themselves and proud of their achievements. Praising people around you in an authentic and relevant manner is incredibly powerful and for me is an indication of emotional intelligence. Authentic praise leaves a lasting impression on both the giver and the receiver and is a sure sign of the ability to perceive the emotional needs of others. A person with high emotional intelligence does this consistently and authentically as they understand the emotional lift it provides the receiver, especially within a group context. An emotionally intelligent person focuses more on others than on themselves and therefore uses authentic praise to positively influence those around them.

Sir Richard Branson, the founder of the Virgin Group, is a firm believer in the importance of praise within the workplace and regularly speaks about its value. One can see the impact authentic praise has had on his organisation through their rapid success and positive work culture. By praising others, you not only encourage them in their work, but you also build long-lasting emotional connections that are the foundation of rapport.

Authentic praise is an important pillar of emotional intelligence as it indicates a focus on others. At the heart of emotional intelligence is a confidence and assuredness in one's own abilities and attributes, and the ability to highlight the positives in others is evidence of this. People with high emotional intelligence do not require constant praise or positive input as they are confident in who they are. Instead, they are able to provide authentic praise to those around them as there is a confidence deep within themselves, and their focus is outward-looking.

Pillar Five — Resisting Impulsivity and Demonstrating Composure

Taking time to pause, breathe and then act when faced with challenging scenarios demonstrates emotional intelligence. It allows you time to identify your emotions, regulate them and then respond in the most appropriate way. People who respond hastily without pausing to consider the ramifications or impact of their words or actions can often get themselves into tricky situations. There are countless examples where rapport has been lost between people due to a comment or reaction made "in the heat of the moment". Emotionally intelligent people don't let unregulated emotional reactions negatively impact their rapport with others. Instead, they demonstrate patience and composure as they pause, breathe, and then act when faced with challenging situations. Nothing displays emotional intelligence and composure more than a well-articulated response or action that is not an unregulated emotional reaction. No matter what the context, always pause, take a breath and then respond. According to Daniel Goleman, the widely-recognised founder of the emotional intelligence movement, *"There is perhaps no psychological skill more fundamental than resisting impulse."* The ability to resist impulsive, unregulated emotional reactions is a sure sign of heightened emotional intelligence.

Reflecting on the Five Pillars

I encourage you to take time at the end of every day to reflect on your actions and interactions. During this process of reflection, use the five pillars of emotional intelligence as a checklist. You will very quickly be able to identify pillars in which you are strong and ones that require intentional action to develop. Be honest with yourself and evaluate how many of the pillars you put into practice in an authentic way throughout the day. As a reflection tool, the five pillars will provide you with a framework with which to evaluate your level of emotional intelligence. While all of these pillars require intentionality, they will flow more naturally from a person with high emotional intelligence. As you reflect on them be honest with yourself and use them to gain perspective on your level of emotional intelligence.

A person's emotional intelligence is influenced by many factors and there is not one formula as to why a person is emotionally intelligent. However, one factor that does influence emotional intelligence is a person's upbringing, including the relationship with their immediate family members, the culture in which they were raised, and their ongoing relationships and personal struggles. As children we model our human interactions on what we see and interactions form a large part of emotional intelligence. These observations in a person's youth will form the foundation of the manner in which they interact throughout their adult life. The context in which we spend our formative years will therefore play a big role in how we view emotions and people. However, it is very important to know that emotional intelligence can be developed, just like any other skill, through a process of gaining awareness and intentional action. Every human being can and should be intentionally developing their understanding of emotional intelligence as this is increasingly becoming the sought-after attribute employers look for. Cognitive ability is important, but it will only take a person so far in their professional life. High emotional intelligence, on the other hand, will blow the lid off a person's potential.

So when you are intentional about living out the five pillars of emotional intelligence every day, your emotional intelligence will develop quickly.

Not only are the five pillars evidence of emotional intelligence, they are also a roadmap to increasing one's ability to connect with others. People will see you differently and your ability to build authentic rapport with people will increase. Emotional intelligence requires action, and in order to develop it one needs to practice it as one would any other skill. Invest in yourself by taking time every day to work on understanding your emotions and then developing the ability to regulate them effectively. I encourage you again to do the exercise mentioned in this chapter everyday as I know it has the potential to develop a deep connection with your emotions.

Professional Perspective
— Maxine Driscoll, Geelong, Australia

Hi there, my name is Maxine Driscoll and I have been a passionate leader in one way or another for over 20 years. Much of my leadership experience comes from leading International Baccalaureate schools in Australia and Asia; being a board member on several profit and not-for-profit organisations; and launching myself into the corporate world as an entrepreneur.

In all these endeavours I have learnt a great deal about leadership.

Leading others is always fraught with challenge and difficulty; however, if we approach our experiences and contexts with a growth mindset we can learn and grow into a better leader and better version of ourselves. How fabulous is that?

I've learnt that building genuine rapport with others and developing authentic relationships is paramount in any leadership role. Actually, I believe that contemporary leaders must possess high-level emotional intelligence (EQ) skills, to lead and empower others.

Daniel Goleman's work on emotional intelligence has been a fabulous asset to me. Being self-aware and self-managing is only half of the leadership challenge. Relationship management, requiring social awareness and social skills, ensures that you will always lead teams and organisations with high levels of rapport. These skills will develop the trust and confidence of your teams, allowing you to inspire, empower, create shared goals, and be a positive change catalyst and visionary innovator.

If you are interested, you can learn more about my leadership journey on my blog www.thinkstrategicforschools.com/blog or you might like to check out my new book *Leadership Really Matters*.

Whatever your leadership journey I think the wise words of Paulo Freire, in his book, *Pedagogy of the Oppressed*, are always worth considering: "The biggest pitfall for a leader is to be for people or worse above people." Freire's whole philosophy of leadership is "to be with people but still lead them". I have based my 20 years of leadership on authenticity and the same principles as Freire.

Maxine Driscoll
Founder & CEO
Think Strategic

Chapter Four

Strategies to Build Rapport

"Rapport leads to connection, connection leads to relationship, and relationship leads to trust." Mike Gilmour

In the opening chapters of this book we laid the foundation of what rapport truly is. I hope that by now you are convinced of the power of rapport and its essential role in forming organisational culture and personal connections. We will now move on to the practical part of the book and discover how you can develop the ability to build rapport in your own life. Each chapter from now on will relate to a specific strategy that you can use to become better at building rapport. However, it is important to note that building rapport is not a simple turnkey solution that can mechanically lead to your desired outcome. Rapport is about individuality and has to be authentic in order to achieve results. Quite simply, you need a genuine interest in the other person for your efforts to be authentic. While the strategies you will read about in the coming chapters will help you practically develop your ability to build rapport, they will mean very little without a genuine care for people. Authenticity is the starting point.

However, before we begin looking at the practical steps you can take to develop your ability to build rapport, it is important that you know where these strategies come from. These strategies that you'll read about in the coming chapters are not a random collection of ideas that I stumbled upon. Rather, they are strategies that I have identified, developed and implemented in my life and I have seen their benefits. They are strategies that I have spent time analysing, practising and evaluating as I've moved through my career. Not all of them have worked immediately and I would say that some may be more valuable than others. However, what I want you to know before you begin reading them is that they have helped me to connect more effectively with other people.

Therefore, as you read through the strategies in the coming chapters I want you to know that I have experienced each one of them help me to build rapport with people. I can testify to their effectiveness if developed and implemented consistently. It's worth me also saying at this point that I do not consider myself an expert on relationships. As you've heard in previous chapters, I am passionate about human interactions and have dedicated a large part of my life to understanding them, but I am also well aware that there are many other more qualified people out there. My hope though is that by sharing these strategies that have worked in my life you will experience similar connections in your own life.

While I do believe that these practical strategies will be able to help you connect with people more effectively, I have learnt that human interactions are a very personal thing. Therefore, it is important that you consider your own approach to relationships and rapport as you read the following chapters. Ultimately, while we can learn from one another, every human being needs to figure out the best way that they interact with other people. The following strategies work for me on a daily basis and I'm confident that they will work for you. However, keep in mind that your context may be different and that you may need to change your approach when it comes to some of these strategies.

Now that you have an understanding of rapport, you might be asking: How can I build authentic and effective rapport? Or, what are the practical steps I can take to develop this skill? As already mentioned, building rapport is a skill that requires action. As a manager, leader or colleague you cannot build rapport from your office desk, it is all about interacting with people where they are at, both practically and emotionally. It is a dynamic and exciting process that will have successes and challenges, yet a process that will develop you not only as a professional, but also as an individual.

Most people will respond positively as you implement the strategies outlined in the coming chapters. However, there will always be people who don't. Don't get despondent if people do not respond in the manner you expected. The most important part of this process is to remain consistent and authentic in your approach. Remember, developing rapport is a skill which anyone can learn. If you dedicate time to this skill you will find your ability to connect with others will dramatically increase. It's also worth stating that the more time you invest into this process, the greater success you will experience in the future. Building rapport is an ongoing journey of discovery and through this process you will be prompted to regularly reflect on your thoughts and actions. As you reflect on your own understanding and ability to build rapport, you will increase your understanding and awareness of human connections. This increased awareness will lead to a greater ability to regulate your actions. Increased awareness leads to increased regulation.

There are six strategies that will help you build rapport and enhance your working environment. You will see that each strategy covered has a practical component within the chapter. Take time to reflect on your understanding while reviewing each strategy in order to assess if this is an area of strength or development for you. Use the practical exercises along the way to reinforce your understanding, and gain an awareness of your current abilities. Once you have worked through all six strategies, you will then be guided through an action plan in the last chapter. The purpose of the action plan is implementation. So often people read books or attend conferences but fail to implement what they have learnt. I encourage you to dedicate time to your action plan and begin to implement these six strategies as you gain awareness through reading the upcoming chapters. This will help you make the changes that you need to as you journey through this book.

CHAPTER FIVE

STRATEGY ONE: BODY LANGUAGE

"Your body language shapes who you are." Amy Cuddy

For a large part of my career I have worked in the education industry. I consider working in education a privilege as it is the ultimate training ground for the real world. While there are a wide range of educational beliefs, pedagogies, contexts and models, at its absolute core is a commitment to the transfer of knowledge and skills from one generation to another. This process of gaining understanding and knowledge that takes place every day in schools intrigues me, as there are many ways in which it can be achieved. There is not one correct way to teach children. However, there are definitely correct ways within each context that lead to effective teaching and learning. Another aspect of education that intrigues me is the connection between student performance and rapport. There have been many research papers written about the influence the human connection between a student and a teacher has on a student's academic progression. All of these research papers point categorically towards higher academic attainment levels where students and their teachers have an authentic connection.

Why am I talking about education at the start of a chapter on body language? Well, quite simply, I'd like to tell you a story about how I used my understanding of body language to become a better educator.

Many years ago I was working as an educator in an international school in Asia. This particular school had students enrolled from many countries around the world. In fact, each classroom resembled something close to the United Nations general assembly! Hearing five or six different languages spoken as I walked through the school corridors was not uncommon. It was an exciting and dynamic environment in which to work and managing the various cultures and perspectives while trying to teach the curriculum was both a challenge and a privilege. I was privileged to have so many fantastic students in my classes at that time and I believe they taught me as much as I taught them. During one year in particular there were two students in my class who on the surface seemed to have similar personalities. However, as I got to know them better in class throughout the year, I realised how different they were and how my approach to each of them needed to be differentiated. As an educator one of our primary responsibilities is to understand each student's learning style and needs. Once an educator has a deep understanding of each of their student's learning abilities they can then structure their lessons in such a way that meets all the needs in the classroom. This is by no means an easy task and I take my hat off to all the educators out there!

To protect the students' identity, I'll call the first student Rob* and the second student Paul*. Here's a bit about them: Rob was a highly talented student who was often misunderstood. His enthusiasm, independence and strong will sometimes led him into misunderstandings or tricky situations with other students. However, he was a logical and kind student who would take great delight in 'simply' explaining complex concepts or solutions to whoever needed help. Rob had a presence about him from day one, and a loud voice, and so everyone knew when he was around or when he arrived.

Paul on the other hand began the school year quietly, but quickly became a very popular student as he grew in confidence during the school year. He was a conscientious student who would diligently do his work, although at times he found it challenging. He was a social student and had many friends, but initially didn't stand out too much and just seemed like another happy, kind and engaged student. But as the year progressed his gregarious personality would see him become highly influential in our class and school.

So why am I telling you about these two students? Well, as I taught these students throughout the year I learnt to assess their level of engagement simply by looking at their body language. For some reason they would display their level of engagement more dramatically through their body language than the other students in my class. Now just to be clear, I believe that every human being displays their emotional state through their body language. This fact emphasises the connection between our emotions and our bodies. However, some people tend to display this more dramatically than others. These two students definitely expressed themselves more through their actions, while some of my other students would express themselves verbally or in other ways. As the year went on and as I taught these students in my class I gained an accurate insight into their world from the way they stood, how they moved or how they interacted with their peers. This was a real lesson for me and highlighted how important body language is in every context. It is the ultimate litmus test for a human being's emotional state. So whether it is gaining an understanding of one's own body language, or developing the ability to read another person's body language, it is an essential tool in building rapport.

As the year went by I learnt to base my teaching to these students largely in response to the body language they displayed. Often, but not always, their body language told me a message that they sometimes did not verbalise. For example, their level of engagement in a particular subject would often be evidenced through their physical demeanour.

As a teacher I found this strategy to be very helpful to my purpose, which was to educate all of my students. This was a great lesson in body language for me and another example of how influential a person's body language is to those around them. We often underestimate how much information can be gained from observing a person's body language. In this situation I was able to become a better teacher to all of my students because I learnt the importance of body language and how to read it effectively.

Both Rob and Paul moved back to their home countries with their families shortly after I taught them and I'm very confident that they will be highly successful in life. Perhaps you have a similar experience around body language that you can reflect on as you read this chapter.

What Exactly Is Body Language?

When I speak about body language I am referring to all non-verbal communication that a person uses to express their feelings and emotions. Most elements of body language happen without us being consciously aware of them. A person's body language is their body's natural physical response to their emotional state. Over time it can become a learned behaviour. A person can actively change their body language by understanding its influence on those around them and by being intentional about how they use it. Awareness leads to regulation, and as you become aware of your body's conscious or subconscious actions you will be able to regulate them and ensure your body is communicating the message you want it to.

Many people aren't aware of this, but our body language communicates around 50 to 70 percent of our daily communication. However, for many of us our body language is unregulated as we are not aware of the importance of it in our daily communication. We simply don't consider it as we go through our daily lives. Our body language expresses our emotional state subconsciously and without awareness of this we may be communicating a message that we do not intend to communicate. Many people go about their daily lives blissfully unaware of the influence their body language is having on those around them. People very quickly form an opinion of us based largely on our body language, so gaining an awareness of how you carry yourself is a key step in building the ability to establish rapport.

Consider for a minute what it would be like if we were constantly aware of our body language, aware of how we moved and the message these physical actions communicated to others? What if we considered our facial expressions while in conversation with others, or used our hand gestures to build trust? What if we had the ability to use our body language as a powerful tool with which to build rapport and develop human connections? The good news is that you *do* have the power to control your body language. It all starts with awareness. Being aware of the importance of body language and how influential it can be when interacting with others is the starting point in this process. As your awareness of your body language increases, so too will your ability to regulate it. It is only when you have developed the ability to regulate your body language, regardless of your emotional state, that you will be able to use it as a strategy to build rapport with others.

I often cringe when watching people's body language, especially if it is negative and they are unaware of the unintended message it is broadcasting to those around them. A small change here or there can completely alter the message your body language sends to people in your presence. It all comes back to gaining an awareness of your current body language. By the way, you're going to hear me say a lot about awareness in the following chapters as I really believe that we cannot change our behaviour and actions without an awareness of what we currently do.

If a person has gained awareness of their body language and developed the ability to regulate it, regardless of their emotional state or level of stress, they will be in control of most of the communication they express every day through their body. Obviously, you can regulate your verbal communication, but if this is only 30 to 50 percent of your daily communication, what are you unintentionally communicating the rest of the day? If you are going to build authentic and effective rapport with people you will have to gain awareness of your body language and master the ability to regulate it. But, like any skill, it takes practice.

Practical Exercise — Gaining Awareness

Here is a quick practical exercise you can begin with to develop an awareness of your body language. Practice it daily and you will stimulate your conscious and subconscious brain to develop an awareness of your body language.

Step One

Find a comfortable chair in a quiet space where you can sit with your eyes closed.. Once you have sat quietly for a minute, begin thinking about your body. What does it feel like right now? Try and connect your thoughts with your body and then speak the answer out aloud. Your answer might be "relaxed", "comfortable", "tense", "tired". These are real feelings. Acknowledge them. The purpose of this step is to begin to connect a word with the feeling in your body. This exercise is fairly similar to the emotional awareness exercise in the earlier chapters. Remain in this reflective state for a few minutes as you identify what you physically feel in your body.

Step Two

While you sit in a relaxed and quiet space, visualise a time in the last 48 hours when you felt happy, excited or positive. Dwell on this image and really try to immerse yourself in it. Now as you are visualising that emotional feeling, try to identify what you are physically feeling in your body. Is there a physical response to the emotional feeling you get when you visualise those scenarios? Initially you might not feel anything, but keep visualising the scenario and keep asking yourself what your body feels as you recall emotional situations. Once you have a word to describe what you feel physically, speak it out. These are the physical feelings I want you to identify. This process will begin to connect how your body feels within a certain emotion or experience, establishing an awareness of the connection between your emotions and your body.

The purpose of this brief exercise is to help you connect your emotions with a feeling in your body. Without a doubt there is a connection between what we feel in our *emotions* and what we feel in our *bodies*. A perfect example to prove this is the physical impact stress or anxiety has on our bodies. Aches and pains, headaches, fatigue, and high blood pressure are just some examples that come to mind. Similarly, the positive emotions we feel result in positive influences in our bodies. Therefore, being able to reflect on your emotions through a prior experience and connect that emotion with a feeling in your body is an important connection to make. Over time I've learned how my body responds to my emotions and feelings, and I can then regulate my physical actions accordingly.

Perhaps you are experiencing similar feelings in your body in response to the emotion you are visualising. It is important to remember that when visualising your emotional state during a positive or negative event, you are describing the feeling in your body, not the emotions you are feeling. It may take some time to be able to identify what you are feeling physically, but keep at it. Awareness is a skill developed over time and will lead to an understanding of the connection between your emotions and your body.

All our emotional energy, both positive and negative, is stored within our body. This is why people cry or scream when faced with an overwhelming situation. Being able to identify what your emotions physically feel like is very important as this link will allow you to regulate your actions irrespective of your emotional state. Remember, the first step towards regulation is *awareness*. Therefore, work on gaining an awareness of how your body feels as you experience various emotions. Descriptive words such as lightness, fresh, relaxed, powerful, confident, and bold are often associated with positive emotions and experiences. Conversely, people often describe the physical feelings of negative emotions as twisted, tight, weak, energy-less, distant, or lethargic. As you experience a range of emotions every day, your body responds through movement, posture and position. The most successful people I know understand the connection between their emotions and body language and are therefore intentional about regulating the message their body language portrays in spite of their emotional state. Perhaps you've never even considered the message your body language is portraying. But I hope that you are starting to understand the importance of this aspect of your daily communication.

What is the Connection Between Body Language and Rapport?

Communication is ultimately at the heart of the rapport-building process, and as we have seen earlier in this chapter, nonverbal communication communicates far more to others than our voices do. Therefore, body language plays an integral role in building rapport as communication is a key component of rapport. Remember, people will observe what you *do* way more than what you *say*, and so without the ability to regulate, or control your body language you could be sending mixed messages that raise uncertainty levels. And one of the first priorities when building rapport is to lower uncertainty levels. This is why the ability to understand and regulate your body language is critical for rapport.

I believe there are five body language essentials that I have found build trust and rapport in any situation. By authentically implementing these essentials you will portray a positive message through your body language. Coupled with intentional messaging through your actions, you will be on track to body language mastery. Take your time to read through each body language essential and look to apply it to your daily actions and interactions. If you find that you are currently doing some of these body language essentials, great! If that's the case continue to reflect on your body language and how you could continue to enhance the message your body portrays.

1. Smile

Many people consider smiling to be a purely involuntary reaction to experiences that bring a person joy and happiness. The truth is that smiling can be just as much a voluntary action displayed through conscious choice as an involuntary response. There are many studies that highlight the benefits of smiling, but for me the most powerful consensus is that smiling is attractive to others and benefits one's own health and wellbeing. Smiling is more than simply manipulating your facial muscles. Smiling is a window into your world that invites people in. It is a simple gesture that tells others a lot about your attitude and posture towards them. Smiling is often associated with warmth, friendliness, openness, integrity, honesty... and the list goes on. These attributes associated with smiling have been proven to be attractive to people and vital in the rapport-developing process. Without a doubt, people who smile more will have a greater advantage when connecting with others.

If you make a conscious effort to smile I guarantee that your interactions with your colleagues will improve. People are attracted to smilers. There is an intrinsic and emotional connection that takes place when people smile at each other. I really believe that if you smile regularly and genuinely throughout the day, regardless of your current emotional state, you will lay the foundation for great rapport. However, remember that your smile should be real... fake smiles are just awkward!

Smiling is both voluntary and involuntary, so it is important to take time throughout your day to reflect on your facial expressions. Ask yourself: What does my facial expression say about me now? Am I portraying a positive disposition to others at the moment? If smiling doesn't come naturally to you, make a conscious effort to smile more. It's okay to be intentional about this, but, I hear you saying, what if you are having a bad day? This is a very valid point as you will not involuntarily smile if you are experiencing a negative emotion. However, experience has shown me that intentionally smiling can actually shift my emotional state and perspective from negative to positive. It's almost like you have to demonstrate the emotion you want before you experience it. I understand that this is not always easy, but give it a try sometime. In the midst of a negative experience, smile. I'm very confident your emotional state will begin to shift.

Now before you think that I'm a person who never experiences negative emotions, it's important to know that there will definitely be days where you don't feel like smiling. That is okay, it is life. But it is on days like these that you need to be intentional about smiling in order to portray a consistent message to others. You might not want to high five people in the hallway, or talk to everyone you see, but you can always offer a simple smile, regardless of how you feel.

2. Walk Tall

The way you carry yourself while walking, sitting or standing tells people a lot about you. When people find themselves in emotionally stressful situations, it manifests in their bodies, often in a hunched over or lethargic stance. In addition to times of stress or negativity, the way we stand and move can become a habit requiring correction if it does not express the appropriate message. Standing tall declares confidence and positivity to others. It is possible to train your body to move in a certain way in order to portray a certain message. And like any other learnt behaviour, this too can become a habit. People observe how you stand and move with both their conscious and subconscious brain, forming an opinion of you. By standing tall and moving with confidence, people will be drawn to you, which allows you to develop rapport. High energy levels, positivity and confidence are attractive attributes which people link to the profile they have of you in their brain. By intentionally walking tall you will exude these attributes and form a positive impression in people's minds.

Initially it will be hard to retrain your body, especially if you identify big changes that are required, but after three to four weeks of consistent and intentional action you will develop new patterns of behaviour and movement. Remember, regulation begins with awareness. Reflect on your body stance regularly and develop awareness throughout the day of how you move by asking yourself, "What is my body position saying now?" As this process of reflection becomes natural you will gain a constant awareness of your body position and then you will be able to regulate your body accordingly. The greater your level of awareness is, the greater your ability to regulate will become.

3. Move with Purpose

Following on from standing tall, it is important to move with purpose throughout your day. I describe moving with purpose as a demonstration of energy on the move. We all know that one colleague who moves around the workplace like a sloth. If you think about them, do words like positive, energetic, or confident come to mind? Probably not, instead, you might describe them as lazy, ineffective or possibly even negative. Our bodies reveal more about us to others than our words do and so considering how we move is vitally important.

Now think about yourself. How do you think people would describe you based on how you move? Are you lethargic in your movements or is there a spring in your step? Do you inspire energy, positivity and confidence as you move? Believe it or not, you can inspire these attributes in others through the way you move. As mentioned previously, people are attracted to high energy levels, positivity and confidence. By moving with purpose and displaying these three attributes through your body as you move every day, regardless of your emotional state or level of fatigue, you will draw people to yourself and find it easier to build connections.

But before we move on to the fourth body language essential, here is an important disclaimer. Move with purpose, but have time for everyone. It is essential to strike a balance; you don't want people to see you as too busy or always rushed. Moving with purpose is more about the *way* in which you move than the *speed* with which you move. Have a clear purpose in your mind, move with intent and demonstrate high energy levels, positivity and confidence, and people will be drawn to you. This is a vital step in building rapport and one which you can control easily.

4. Reflect and Regulate Constantly

Retraining your body is never easy, but I firmly believe that reflection is a powerful tool to help you gain awareness and understanding of all areas in your life. In order to consistently demonstrate positive body language you need to master the art of constant reflection. Being able to reflect while actively engaged in another task is not easy, but when rapport and body language are at the forefront of your mind, it becomes easier. Regularly ask yourself, "What message am I communicating through my body?" This simple reflective question will help you to regulate your body stance or posture if necessary. I tend to ask myself this question several times throughout the day. Whether I'm in conversation with someone, walking through the corridor or in a board meeting, this simple question quickly causes me to reflect on my current body language and then make any adjustments required.

As you reflect on your movements and non-verbal communication you will gain an awareness of your body language. You can then regulate your movements accordingly so that you broadcast the positive non-verbal message intended. You should be regularly reflecting on your non-verbal communication by trying to see yourself from another person's perspective. This process of reflection and regulation takes practice, but as body language is so powerful in building rapport, it is essential.

5. Personal Space

Finally we come to the fifth body language essential. This is more about body awareness than body language. However, the two are closely related and the understanding of personal space is critically important to building rapport.

Let's be honest, we all know someone who stands too close during a conversation. So close that you can see the finer details of their face and intricate details of their morning shaving routine. These people often tend to be blissfully unaware of the awkward position they are putting the other person in. In a conversation where someone is a 'space invader' the focus of the other person is more on how to escape than on the content of the conversation. Reflect for a minute if you've ever been in a situation like this. Did you enjoy conversing with that person who was too close? Or perhaps you didn't even have a conversation, you might have experienced someone invading your personal space while standing in a line at the grocery store. How did you feel? I remember one time standing in the line in a grocery store in Cape Town and the guy behind me was so close I could feel his breath on the back of my neck whenever he exhaled! No matter how much further forward I crept, he followed me and the breathing continued! Thank goodness I didn't have too much longer to wait before I paid and got out. Thanks to this experience I am very aware of where I now stand when shopping.

Regardless of how engaging or likeable a person may be, most people do not enjoy having their personal space invaded. There is something about our energy levels, personal space and sense of hygiene that waves red flags, so we look for the quickest possible exit to the conversation. We have all been there in some way or another.

Space-invading is a rapport killer and needs to be avoided at all costs. Avoid being this person by reflecting on how others respond to you while in conversation. Do people you converse with often pull away from conversations with you? Do you find people backing away slowly as you engage with them? Reflecting on people's behaviour while they talk to you is one way you can assess if you are a personal-space invader. Another way to assess this is simply to ask a few trusted friends for their honest opinion of you. The sooner you know about it and can correct it, the sooner you will see higher levels of engagement with others. Now it must be said that generally most people tend to know where the personal space boundaries are and those who don't are in the minority. So while this is not a problem for most people, it is still vital to gain an awareness of whether you are guilty of this or not.

However, I am aware that the unspoken rules that govern personal space vary according to culture. In some cultures it is seen as offensive if you are not interacting closely with another person. You need to look at the culture in which you live and seek to understand what is generally accepted in terms of personal space. Spend time observing and reflecting on the culture in which you work and then on your actions while interacting with others.

As you reflect and practice these positive body language essentials, you will notice a change in the way people interact with you. As you harness and use your body's non-verbal communication to communicate a positive message to those around you, you will notice people changing their attitude towards you. I am very confident of this. They will become more open to you and more responsive to your interactions. This is such a critical element in building rapport. Understand how your body language works and use your body to make an impact on people and communicate the message that you want to communicate.

Exercise Two - Understanding Your Body Language

Earlier in this chapter you completed a visualisation exercise that helped you identify the physical responses to the emotions you experience. It is an important awareness exercise that should be repeated daily. Now I would like to focus on a practical exercise that will assist you to gain an awareness of your body language while you are interacting with people. It can be implemented wherever you are and with whomever you are interacting.

Step One:

You are now going to learn how to regulate your body language while in conversation with someone. For this exercise you will need to initiate a conversation with someone. During the conversation ask yourself: what message is my body communicating? And while remaining present in the conversation, allow your brain to reflect on this for a moment. Then, as you are conversing, adjust your body using the first two positive body language essentials. Smile and stand tall. These two adjustments will not only change the way you are verbally communicating, they will also change the way the other person responds in conversation. Try to identify any changes you see in the other person as a result of you regulating your body language during conversation.

Step Two:

The next thing I would like you to do while in conversation is to use your body to connect and influence the body of the other person. This technique is known as mirroring. So here is what you do. As you are speaking to them fold your arms in front of you and continue the conversation. You may find the person you are speaking to will also fold their arms. If this happens, once they have copied your body position then place your hands on your hips or in another position and quickly watch them follow your actions. I have always found that the greater my emotional connection is with the person, the greater the likelihood is of them following my physical actions.

Mirroring is a strategy you can use when speaking to someone who has a negative body language. You might find them somewhat closed to what you are saying or asking, but as you influence their body language you can also influence a greater openness and receptivity to your message. As we have learnt earlier in this book, there is a connection between a person's body and their emotional state. I always like to stand or sit in an 'open' position when in conversation. My hands are by my side or in another comfortable position, which invites an open conversation. People in a 'closed' position often have their arms folded or have their shoulders turned inwardly. By positively influencing the body language of the person you are speaking with, you will greatly increase your ability to connect with them. It's important to understand that people almost always enter conversations with residue from prior conversations or interactions. You don't want this potential negativity from a prior experience to influence your conversation or ability to connect.

Awareness is the beginning of regulation; you will hear this phrase many times throughout the book as it truly is the cornerstone of a person's ability to build rapport. Through the two exercises in this chapter, as well as the five positive body language essentials, you will be able to develop an awareness of what message your body communicates to those around you. With this growing awareness you will be able to regulate your body movements and positions in order to communicate your desired message. Positive body language is both voluntary and involuntary and therefore, like any skill, requires practice to master. Take time every day to work on these two exercises and you will see your body language change and your ability to connect with others increase. A positive body language is essential in the rapport-building process. Do not overlook the impact your non-verbal communication has on others.

Professional Perspective
- Craig Kemp, Nelson, New Zealand

As an educator, school leader and global EdTech consultant now for more than 13 years I have been lucky enough to work with hundreds of schools in countries all over the globe. When I walk into a school the culture is the first thing that I notice and the most identifiable part of this culture is the rapport people have with each other. From body language and actions to spoken words, rapport means a lot in education, whether it is from educators to students, to parents or to colleagues it is a critical element that underpins the success of an organisation.

As a young educator in New Zealand my mentor once gave me this advice that I live by today: "There is nothing more important here than relationships. Relationships mean everything. Spend your first year building relationships with everyone you come across and you will be successful". This is something I always have in the back of my mind during every interaction, whether inside my workplace or not.

Now as a leader and EdTech consultant with schools I always start with the importance of rapport. I spend time to get to know people and allow them an insight into who I am by sharing stories that connect; personal stories that are genuine and something that people can attach themselves too. This time investment goes a long way when developing long-term relationships to ensure the success of a project or activity.

Craig Kemp
mrkempnz.com
@mrkempnz

Chapter Six

Strategy Two: Communication

"Communication — the human connection — is the key to personal and career success." Paul J. Meyer

Following on from non-verbal communication, we will now turn our attention to the impact verbal communication has on building rapport. Communication has a massive influence on our ability to build rapport and connect with others. Verbal communication, together with one's body language, is the primary means you use to build a relationship and therefore a connection. Through verbal communication you connect with people by saying the right thing at the right time or by instilling trust with the words you speak. You give people a window into your world through your words, and allow them to either trust you or not. I am a firm believer that effective verbal communication can solve many of the world's problems. Whether it is an issue between two people or two countries, the ability we have to talk things out, come to a consensus and then form a deeper understanding with one another relies on our ability to verbally communicate. If used effectively, verbal communication is a tremendous tool for building rapport.

Sadly, many people these days lack the ability to verbally communicate effectively. While the rapid speed of technology development aids our world in so many ways, it arguably also reduces essential skills such as verbal communication. During my time in various leadership positions, I have been amazed at how many employees struggle when it comes to verbal communication. A simple conversation around a contentious issue or a public speaking opportunity are often met with high levels of anxiety and stress as people have not developed the communication skills required to manage these opportunities effectively. Becoming a good communicator is an intentional act which requires consistent dedication and practice. And like developing most skills, there will be many failures along the way, but those failures teach us valuable lessons and lead to progress.

Public speaking is one example of verbal communication that a lot of people struggle with. To be honest, I used to fear speaking to crowds of people. During these times on stage every insecurity in my life would surface and I would find them highly stressful situations. I remember one experience in elementary school where I had to read out a list of announcements in the school assembly. I don't think I slept much the night before as fear and anxiety gripped me. During the speech I remember my hands sweating and shaking and my inconsistent breathing not allowing me to read the announcements clearly. It was a terrible experience and I couldn't wait for it to be over. However, fairly early on in my career I knew that I wanted to be a leader and I knew that public speaking was an essential part of this role. So I made a decision to change my mentality around public speaking. I began to use positive words and phrases when speaking about my ability to speak in public. I built confidence in myself through the words I spoke and limited any negative connotations around public speaking. I am a big believer in speaking positive words over your life as I know the change it influences. Over time I noticed that my anxiety around public speaking was reducing significantly and a new confidence grew within me. This reduced anxiety and lots of experience on stage helped me become a lot more effective as a public speaker. Nowadays I actually love speaking publicly and enjoy the challenge of delivering a message in a clear and confident manner. My advice to people struggling with public speaking is to begin speaking positive words over their life about their ability to speak publicly. For example, one could say, "I am a confident public speaker". A simple phrase like this, repeated daily, can have a huge impact on your confidence levels and will force any negativity aside. Actually, I still speak positive phrases like this one before I speak on stage and I find it is a huge help. And, obviously, in addition to the positive pep talk you can give yourself, becoming better at public speaking also has a lot to do with experience. The more you do it, the more comfortable you will become. So the next time you're offered an opportunity to speak publicly, say yes!

Anyway, enough about public speaking, let's get back to verbal communication. How, when and why you communicate will determine the efficacy of your verbal communication and therefore, your ability to build rapport. The right word spoken at the right time can completely change someone's day, possibly even life. So it is vital that you firstly understand how important verbal communication is, and secondly, develop the ability to speak the words people need to hear, regardless of context. Remember, rapport is the process of developing an emotional connection with people. Therefore your words always need to initiate or sustain an emotional connection. This is the role of verbal communication in building rapport.

No matter how influential or powerful a person is, everyone has an intrinsic desire to be heard, to be listened to, and to be understood. Once we understand this, the next step is to become highly effective with our spoken communication, so that all of our words are directed towards our intended outcome — building rapport. Begin to evaluate the words you speak each day. Spoken words can either build someone up or tear them down in an instant. Make the intentional choice every day to use your verbal communication as your biggest rapport-building asset. Ask yourself: do my words lift people's emotions and elicit a connection, or do they pull people down and divide? Some honest feedback from those you regularly interact with can help you reflect on your verbal communication. Never be afraid to ask for feedback.

Communicating to the Heart

With the understanding of how important verbal communication is in building rapport, how do we use our spoken words as a tool to build rapport? Firstly, it is vital that you view every conversation, whether casual or professional, as an opportunity to build connections with people. When you approach conversations from this perspective you automatically become intentional about how and what you communicate. Your ear becomes more acutely tuned to listen during conversations so that you can respond in a way that builds a connection. People often view communication simply as a transfer of information from one person to another. They see it as a transactional interaction, which results in both relevant and irrelevant content being shared between people. However, by viewing communication in this light you will not only be less effective in your communication, but you will also be missing a major opportunity to build rapport.

When a person understands that every word they speak has the power to build connections with people, they view verbal communication very differently. They become intentional about using their words appropriately and strategically in order to establish or sustain emotional connections. I like to call it communicating to the heart, as you are no longer simply communicating to transfer information. You are speaking with the intention of building an emotional connection. Don't get me wrong, verbal communication is very much about the transfer of information, and so having the ability to concisely articulate your message in a range of contexts is important. However, when we understand that the manner in which we speak, and the choice of words we use to convey a specific message, can build authentic connections we then approach conversations more intentionally.

Every morning I make a conscious choice to use every interaction I have throughout the day as an opportunity to build rapport. This means that I am intentional about using my spoken words in every conversation to achieve my purpose, which is to build authentic rapport. I don't get this right every time, but that doesn't stop me from being intentional with my spoken words. As a leader I have to regularly have tough conversations with people, and they're not always light and fluffy. There are times when I have to be very direct with my verbal communication. However, I have found that even in these situations the manner in which I use my verbal communication can contribute to a connection. So don't think that only lighthearted conversation can build rapport. This is not realistic. You will leave a greater impression on someone when you turn a challenging conversation into a connection with the right approach and the words you use. So, make the choice to be intentional about using your words every day to speak to a person's heart in order to build rapport.

Listen to Understand

Communication is not only a key component in building rapport; it is also at the heart of community. A community is essentially a group of individuals living independent lives yet connected through a commonality. This commonality may be physical, such as a geographic location, or it can be more conceptual, such as an ideology or belief system. Either way there are always commonalities that connect a community. But making a community function requires communication; it is effectively the engine that drives the connections. However, in today's world where people expect immediate gratification, we are rapidly losing the art of listening earnestly to one another. One only has to observe two people having a disagreement to illustrate my point. People have gotten into the habit of listening to *reply* instead of listening to *understand*.

Listening is a vital element of communication. Actually, without listening one could argue that you are not really communicating, as communication is always a two-way process. So why is listening to *understand* so important? And how does it affect rapport? Remember that everyone has an intrinsic need to be heard and understood. This need will look different from person to person, but the need is indisputably constant. As you look to build rapport with anyone a key strategy is to listen to understand.

Okay, let's be honest for a minute, deep down most humans are selfish. The level of selfishness ranges from person to person, but I'm sure you understand what I mean. It often requires an external factor or an intentional action for a human being to focus on another person. Our desire to be heard often causes us to speak more than we listen. Not listening to understand makes rapport very hard to achieve, so we need to make a conscious effort to pause during conversations and truly listen to the other person. Listening is a selfless act, which requires you to focus on the other person and not yourself. Slow down, listen to understand and then respond once you have truly heard the other person. If you are able to authentically listen to someone you will build a connection with them, as listening shows that your focus is on them.

As we have discussed in previous chapters, it is important to take time to reflect on what you are doing. Remember, awareness is the foundation of regulation, and therefore you cannot adjust your listening habits without becoming aware of what you currently do. To help you in this process, ask five people who you interact with regularly if they feel you are a good listener. Ask them to be honest in their assessment of you; it is the only way you will improve. From the feedback you receive you will know if you are perceived as a good listener or not. Take time to work through this feedback and then adjust your listening habits accordingly.

Exercise Three — Listening to Understand

There are two important steps in becoming a great listener. Firstly, slow down and breathe. Conversations are often fast paced, which exacerbates the problem of not listening. But by intentionally slowing down the pace of the conversation, pausing at the right time before responding, you will allow your brain further time to process what is being heard. Secondly, focus completely on the other person. As you begin a conversation ask yourself: What is this person saying? What do they truly need from me? These questions shift your brain's focus off yourself and onto the other person, allowing you to listen more clearly.

Practice these two steps as you are in conversations today and your awareness of your ability to listen will increase, which will lead to your ability to regulate or change your listening habit.

While we are in the process of reflecting and gaining awareness, think of how often you are introduced to someone and then completely forget their name as soon as you walk away. Remembering names is a skill that requires intentional action and practice until it becomes a habit. A person's name is part of their identity. By remembering someone's name when you address them you place value on that person. It is an incredibly powerful tool to build rapport. It can leave a lasting, positive impression on them and opens the door for authentic rapport. I have noticed how easy it is to build a connection with a relative stranger simply by remembering their name. In many cultures calling someone by their name is the highest sign of respect.

The Power of a Name

In my early twenties while studying at university I had an opportunity to spend a few hours every week volunteering alongside a counsellor in Pollsmoor Prison, one of South Africa's most infamous prisons. The prison was infamous for all the wrong reasons and many people questioned why I would volunteer to serve in this hostile environment where drugs, gangsterism, and physical abuse were rife. I had a gut feeling that this opportunity was meant to be, and that I could have a positive impact on the young people society had largely forgotten.

At the time I was studying my undergraduate degree in sport and exercise science. By chance I met a counsellor who was working in the prison and I was intrigued at the work she was doing. At the time they had need of a volunteer to run a sports program for the inmates and they offered me the opportunity to come in each week for a few hours to work with the inmates. The young men who were in the prison were there for a variety of crimes, and conditions in the prison, as you can imagine, were quite horrific. Overcrowding, drugs, gangsterism, sickness and abuse were daily occurrences that mirrored many of their lives on the outside. However, I knew that through sport I could build connections with these young men and hopefully have a positive influence on them.

The need for social work within the prison system in South Africa is overwhelming due to overcrowding and low funding. Most inmates I worked with lived in a cell with 60 to 70 other inmates. However, the cell was originally designed for only 15 inmates. It was no surprise, therefore, that they were desperate for volunteers who could serve in any way. I viewed this as an amazing opportunity and a privilege. While I wasn't a trained counsellor, I always worked alongside one together with the prison social workers, running sports programs for the inmates. What an eye-opener! Here I was, a young, privileged white university student having grown up in Apartheid South Africa, going into one of South Africa's most violent prisons where the inmate population was nearly one hundred percent people of colour (black and coloured). The warders were severely outnumbered. Often one guard oversaw 250 inmates. I was told that if something went wrong while I was in the cell, it would be a long wait until help arrived. Initially I was so far out of my depth it was embarrassing. Fear would often overtake me. Portraying a sense of confidence and calm was a skill that I had to learn quickly. But over time, and as I built relationships with the inmates and warders, I realised that human beings have so much in common, but our circumstances largely determine our opportunities. I remember speaking to young inmates who had committed horrific crimes and were facing a lifetime in prison, and I couldn't help thinking how similar we actually were. They had dreams, hobbies and passions just like I did. However, due to their circumstances and choices, theirs wouldn't be realised.

During my time serving in the prison, which was about two years, I lead sports programs for hundreds of inmates. You can imagine how hard it was to remember their names. Not only were there hundreds of different faces, but their names were mostly Afrikaans or Xhosa names. It was nearly impossible for me. But I will never forget the advice one of the prison social workers gave me when she saw me struggle week in and week out trying to remember the inmate's names. Her advice stopped me dead in my tracks. "You know Mike," she told me one day, "a name is powerful. For these boys it is all they have. Other than their name, they're simply a number." To this day I have never forgotten her words. A person's name is powerful, regardless of the context, and when remembered you will form an instant connection regardless of what context it is in. Recalling a person's name and using it to address them is a very important element of verbal communication and builds trust with that person.

From that moment I became more intentional about remembering the inmates and warders names. While I couldn't remember everyone's name, I saw the impact it had when I called someone by their name. The connection was instant! This experience was an incredible lesson for me in that it not only humbled me as a person, but it also showed me the value of human connections, even in such trying circumstances. Unfortunately, Pollsmoor Prison remains a very challenging environment for the inmates and warders to this day. However, I am encouraged by the small flickers of hope I see when talking to volunteers still serving in that prison.

With the understanding that remembering people's names is important, it is equally important that we understand how our brain works as we listen to information throughout the day. Our brains are programmed to rapidly recall important information, while information deemed less important may often take longer to recall. So while remembering a name might seem like a small and insignificant action, it plays a huge role in building rapport. You need to be intentional about remembering people's names otherwise your brain will automatically file it as less critical information and therefore make it harder to recall. I have heard many people say to me, "I'm not good with names", or make up similar excuses, and these are often self-fulfilling prophecies. It seems to be an accepted excuse in the world these days and therefore most people aren't intentional about remembering names. By simply being intentional a person can develop the skill of remembering names. It comes back to how much value you place on remembering names and using them in conversation.

Exercise Four - Name Recall

There are many strategies people use to try to remember names, but I find that most actually complicate the process, which is quite simple. This is a simple strategy

I use that I have found to be effective. During the initial conversation, I take the time to look the person in the eye when they are introducing themselves, listen to their name and then I repeat it back to them out loud in the conversation. Here is an example:

Mike: Hi, great to meet you, my name is Mike and welcome to...
Guest: Hi Mike, I'm Simon, thanks for the invite.
Mike: Simon! It's great to have you here.

By speaking the person's name out loud immediately after you have heard it you will greatly increase your brain's ability to recall it in future.

Finally, as you are ending the conversation, say the person's name as you leave. For example:

Mike: So good to meet you Simon, have a great afternoon and we'll be in touch.

As you place the focus of the introductory conversation on the other person and not yourself you will prepare your brain to remember their name and make recall more effective. Remembering someone's name is a powerful strategy with which to build rapport.

Harnessing Paralanguage

Another very important part of verbal communication is paralanguage. Paralanguage relates to verbal communication, but it is everything other than the words you speak. It refers to your intonation, volume, tone and rate of speech, and it has an undeniable influence on the efficacy of the words you speak. Here is a brief breakdown of each aspect of paralanguage:

1. Intonation: Often referred to as pitch, this is the natural highness and lowness of your voice as you speak and the variation in pitch you use.
2. Volume: This refers to the volume of your speech. Are you speaking too loudly or softly?
3. Rate of Speech: This is the speed at which you speak and influences people's ability to accurately hear what you are saying.
4. Tone: This refers to the manner in which you speak and can convey meaning beyond the words that are spoken.

Why is paralanguage important for building rapport? Well, your paralanguage can modify meaning, give nuanced meaning and convey emotion through the words you speak. So not only *what* we say, but also *how* we say it, conveys a message to the listener. Paralanguage can be both conscious and subconscious, and so developing an awareness of your paralanguage is very important if you want to be able to regulate and control the message this part of your speech conveys. By using the brief descriptions above, reflect on your paralanguage during your next conversation and evaluate your intonation (pitch), volume, rate of speech and tone.

In order to become an effective communicator and use your spoken communication to build rapport, you need to develop a consistency between *what* you say and *how* you say it. Let's be honest, no one enjoys listening to a monotone speaker. Being monotonous in your speech is the best way to turn people off or put them to sleep — and no rapport is built while people sleep! You need to match your paralanguage with your spoken message. Imagine delivering a serious message to someone with a high intonation and rate of speech. The paralanguage doesn't match the message. Or imagine trying to instil motivation and energy into an audience, but you speak slowly with a low volume. Once again, there is no consistency between your paralanguage and your message, sending mixed messages to the listener. Remember that most of our daily communication is conveyed without words. While paralanguage is a key part of our verbal communication, it is closely linked to a person's non-verbal communication in that it can convey a subconscious message which at times can be unintended.

In order to help you build rapport your paralanguage and spoken communication need to be aligned. This will lead to a consistency in the message you are delivering and your emotions and intentions will be effectively communicated alongside your spoken words. This is critical to building rapport as mixed messages will create uncertainty in your listeners.

More often than not, a person's paralanguage involuntarily matches the message they intend to communicate. But, if you truly desire to be an effective verbal communicator it is important to reflect on this important aspect of your verbal communication. Awareness is the foundation of regulation and so as you gain an awareness of your spoken communication and paralanguage, your ability to regulate it appropriately will increase.

Before rushing on to the next chapter, take some time to reflect on your paralanguage and whether the way you speak is aligned with the message you speak.

"If you want to build a ship, don't drum up people to collect wood and don't assign them tasks and work, but rather teach them to long for the sea." - Antoine de Saint-Exupéry

I have been involved in leadership teams, sales teams and sports teams around the world for most of my life and have seen some succeed handsomely and others fail dismally. For the last 30 years I have worked with the largest global real estate organisation, which is represented in over 100 countries, and been part of their growth and success. Their ethos and culture was defined by the founders and based on the principle of "Everybody Wins", emphasising the power of building relationships with like-minded people who in turn could lead with a high degree of emotional intelligence.

The global growth was driven by the constant communication of the founders' dream – to build the best, most productive real estate network in the world, an organisation where everybody wins — owners, sales professionals, employees, customers, everybody. The dream was not realised easily and there were many hardships and setbacks along the way, but by listening to the regular feedback and learning from the obstacles, the dream team refined and improved their ideas, extracted benefits and positives, which allowed them to grow and improve.

Ideas capture people's minds but not their hearts. Dreams go to people's hearts and the dream team sold the dream to fully committed team players and convinced them that they too could become part of the dream.

In the words of our founders, "We wanted then — and still want today – to be surrounded by those who buy into the dream as we do, who want it as much as we do, and who are willing to work as hard as we did, with empathy, energy and enthusiasm as we did from the very beginning."

I once heard a saying that said, "God keeps breaking your heart until it opens." Struggles, challenges and adversity bring you closer to your heart, and leadership with heart resulted in our organisation enabling so many people around the world to achieve their dreams.

I am honoured and privileged to have been part of the dream team.

Peter Gilmour
Former Senior Vice President
RE/MAX LLC

CHAPTER SEVEN

STRATEGY THREE: AUTHENTICITY

"Authenticity is at the heart of all things successful." Scott
Dinsmore

Authenticity is the third strategy that we will look at as a means to develop rapport. However, it is important to note that authenticity, while it is definitely a strategy that can be developed, is a characteristic or trait rather than a skill. When it comes to authenticity, a person is constantly evaluated by others through their daily interactions. One cannot learn to be authentic; but a person can learn to display authenticity through their words and actions. Authenticity is often the outward manifestation of a person's inner intentions and is very evident in the way one interacts with others.

Authenticity at its core is being real to who you are, and then displaying that to the world on a daily basis. It is about being honest with oneself and having the confidence to know that your contribution is valid, that there is a purpose to your existence. It is about not putting on a mask that promotes an unreal image or message. Being authentic is about confidently being who you are as you go about your daily life. I have observed that the more assured a person is in the value they bring to the world, the higher their tendency is to be authentic in their interactions with others.

The great athlete Michael Jordan believes *"Authenticity is being true to who you are"*, and I couldn't agree more. The world today is filled with a growing lack of authenticity, as people regularly promote a false image of themselves. One only has to view social media posts to see the lengths people go to in order to promote a perfect picture of their lives. Let's be honest, pictures placed on social media profiles these days are less and less spontaneous and more and more carefully crafted depictions of what society deems to be acceptable. We have created an unattainable standard of perfection where anything below it is deemed a failure. This perpetuates the inaccuracy within our world today and decreases the sense of authenticity within our communities. I believe that at the root of this unattainable perfection is deep insecurity with oneself, and this insecurity is what drives the need to be accepted and the lack of authenticity.

The good news though is that there is a growing hunger for the authentic. Throughout the world today authenticity is increasingly attractive in its stark contrast to the norm. There is something about being authentic that many people are drawn to like a magnet. Perhaps it is because they are able to be themselves and remove the masks they are so often forced to wear. Authenticity is a powerful tool which can build rapport as it releases a freedom within people around you to be themselves too. It removes barriers, disarms conflict and reduces stress. Being authentic empowers those around you to be true to who they are and this allows an emotional connection to take place. As you allow people around you to see who you truly are, failures and all, you will pull down the walls that oppose authenticity in their lives and open a gateway for connection.

An authentic person is someone who is confident to share their opinion even if it is contrary to what others think, as they are true to themselves, rooted in their beliefs. They have a confidence in who they are and are not driven by a need to impress those in their company. Authenticity can't be developed through practice, like a skill, for it is the outward manifestation of a person's inner intentions. However, a person can get better at demonstrating authenticity in their life through their words and actions. A person's lifestyle will naturally reveal their level of authenticity and this will be noticeable to those around them. Authenticity is a characteristic developed over time and is largely influenced by one's personal experience and the value placed upon oneself. Some people identify this value intrinsically while others develop it through their understanding of God or other external factors. Regardless of how a person identifies their inner purpose and value, what we do know is that without it a person will not consistently act in a manner that is authentic. A deep sense of worth is the starting point of authenticity.

I believe that every human being has a level of understanding of their personal worth and therefore a level of authenticity. This is best understood if we place authenticity on a continuum. I have created the Authenticity Continuum to help illustrate this point. The continuum ranges from artificial through to authentic and should be used as a process of self-reflection. Read the questions below and then after you have reflected on your answers, place yourself at a point on the continuum.

Authenticity Continuum

Artificial   Honest   Authentic

Reflection Questions:

- Do you portray a false image of yourself?
- Do you know your life's purpose?
- Do you genuinely value those around you?
- Do you respond well to criticism?

These questions are designed to help you reflect on the level of authenticity you demonstrate within your own life. Once you have reflected for a few minutes place a mark on the continuum where you believe you are at. The way you move along the Authenticity Continuum is to become more at peace with who you are and what your purpose is. As your personal level of certainty increases so too will the public perception of your authenticity.

Every human being is authentic to some degree according to the experience and the value they place upon themselves. So why is this important to rapport? Well, as mentioned earlier, when a person is surrounded by authenticity they will develop authentic attributes through observation and interaction. This is how authenticity influences rapport. It exposes people to something contrary to social norms and they are influenced by it. Think for a minute about the last time you had a deep and honest conversation with someone. Perhaps it was about an issue you were dealing with in your personal life, or a challenge you were facing at work. Now think for a minute how the person you were speaking to responded. Did they open up about some of their challenges? I have experienced this situation countless times and just about every time I speak honestly about a challenge in my life it elicits a similar response from the other person. It's as if my demonstration of authenticity and vulnerability releases an authenticity and honesty in the other person. These examples illustrate how your authenticity influences authenticity in others. Remember, building rapport is more about what you *do* than what you *say*. When you place value on yourself, when you are true to who you are and genuinely want the best for those around you, you will be far along the Authenticity Continuum and people will be drawn to you because of how you make them feel.

Passion for People

"People don't care how much you know, until they know how much you care," says John C. Maxwell. As my career has progressed and I've found myself with an increasing level of responsibility I've come to highly value this quote. For me it really sums up most human interactions, whether in my personal or professional life. As young people I think we often place most of our emphasis on how much we know. This is not necessarily a bad thing as it is often what we know that gets us our first job. In a way, what we know is a manner in which we initially prove our ability to those around us. However, as I have moved through my career and gained experience in various contexts, I have learnt that my knowledge and experience mean very little to people unless I have a connection, or

rapport, with them. It's the human connection and a demonstration of one's ability to care that brings knowledge to life.

Throughout my life I have had many mentors. I believe passionately in mentoring and the ability it has to influence both the mentor and the person being mentored. Therefore, I have actively sought out people who inspire me and I look to learn from them. I can't recommend getting a mentor highly enough as I have experienced the benefits of these relationships first-hand. Anyway, the reason I am telling you about mentors is that I have had many in my life. Some have been formal relationships while others were informal. Either way, my mentors were people who positively built into my life. As a teenager in high school, I remember a few teachers and sports coaches who I identified as mentors. These weren't formal mentoring relationships; in fact they probably didn't even know that I saw them as mentors or role models. However, they had a huge impact on my life because first and foremost I knew how much they cared for me. They demonstrated their care for me in many practical ways, giving up their time to support me, motivating and encouraging me and being present during challenges. It was only because I knew how much they cared for me and believed in me that I responded to their instruction. Without the human connection, their opinion and instruction would've meant very little. It was evident to me that they had a passion for me. If you don't currently have a mentor, or someone you turn to for advice, I encourage you to reach out to someone who you know cares for you and has life experience beyond yours. Whether it is formalised or not, being able to connect with someone who you know has your best interests at heart is highly valuable.

One major contributor to being authentic stems from having a passion for people. You cannot fake this. If you have a genuine interest in people and truly want to make a positive impact in their lives, what you do will be seen and it will be done in an authentic way. Conversely, people who do not have a genuine interest in people try to fake authenticity by their words and actions. Forced authenticity is not only easy to identify, but it is also repulsive. People can see a fake a mile off. I believe putting on an artificial appearance of authenticity is probably one of the most detrimental things a person can do when trying to establish rapport.

When you have a genuine passion for people and an understanding of your value in the world, authenticity is naturally evident in every area of your life. People will see your intentions, and that will create an emotional connection.

As you honestly display your passion for people through your conversations and actions you will develop rapport, if it is authentic. However, if you do not truly have an interest in the well-being of the person you are trying to build rapport with, you will never be seen as authentic. People will see that you are only engaging with them in order to advance your own interests. Authentic rapport is about seeing the best in other people and placing a priority on their needs in that moment. Over time as you consistently place the needs of others above yours you will develop rapport and a strong human connection. People will trust you as you demonstrate and communicate your desire for their success.

Whatever your motive is for wanting to develop rapport, make sure that at the heart of that desire is a passion for people, an authentic longing to see those around you succeed. When you display this passion through your verbal and non-verbal communication and interactions, people will be drawn to you. If you take nothing else from this book, take this: demonstrate your passion for people and your understanding of personal value every day through your words and actions. This alone will provide you with a strong foundation on which to connect with those around you and develop rapport.

Now that you have an understanding of the importance of a passion for people, and the ability to demonstrate it, I'd like to look at another lie we are regularly told.

Celebrate Failure

What? Celebrate failure, surely not...

In society we are told regularly that failure is a direct reflection of who we are. We see this subtle message in advertising campaigns, social media threads and sometimes in workplace culture. As a result of this message people have developed a risk-averse mentality, just in case they make a mistake. The safe option that we are taught is to maintain the status quo, although over time this constant suppression of one's passion and creativity can only lead to long-term dissatisfaction. There are probably thousands of people sitting in offices, schools and industries all over the world today who have brilliant and creative ideas, but they are too scared to try them in case they fail. But failure is not necessarily the end. It is not terminal. Failure simply tells you that what you have just tried does not work in the way you tried it. Failure is the most honest feedback someone can receive, but how a person responds to that feedback is the key to success. Now let's all be honest, no one enjoys failing. But we need to remove our ego from the act of failure. If we do that we will see it as a result of our actions rather than a personal attack on who we are, which can knock us down.

When it comes to failure, it is not only limited to your personal capacity. It is estimated that 90 percent of new product innovations fail. This is a sobering thought. Think about it, each new product we see on the market has often had several rounds of failure before it reached the supermarket shelves. Think about what would have happened if the Wright brothers gave up when their first few aircraft attempts failed. The world may look very different today. Or how about Henry Ford? One of his first cars had no reverse gear! Do you think he found success immediately? Of course not! All of these innovators went through multiple rounds of failure yet kept their gaze fixed on their mission. Without a doubt, the innovations we all enjoy and rely on today, from the personal computer and hand-phone to the motor vehicle and aircraft, would not be as successful if they hadn't failed in their initial stages of development. Failure, if learnt from, will always lead to a better product, understanding or result.

I remember one business failure I went through. I was in my early twenties and a friend and I decided we wanted to start a clothing company. I hear some of you saying, oh yeah, I tried that once! We decided to start with one shirt design, because that's all we could afford, and then if we had success with that we would launch other items. We required little funding to get going and before long had produced our first run of shirts. I think we only made about 50 of them. However, when we tried to sell these shirts by getting them into retail stores we hit a brick wall every time. We thought our shirts were amazing, but no one else did. While thankfully this failure didn't cost us too much of our own money, we did realise that two guys with absolutely no understanding of the textile industry probably shouldn't be launching a clothing company without some guidance. We learnt a lot though this failure and ended up with more than enough unique shirts to see us through our university careers.

You will make mistakes. Whether small or large, they are inevitable. It is important that you get used to that fact, but don't let it shape your sense of value. Obviously everyone wants to limit mistakes and the negative impact they could have on an organisation or individual. This is normal and success should be striven for all the time. However, when you *do* fail it is important that you own it, and then look to learn from it. This is being true to yourself. Like authenticity, when we admit our failures we empower people around us to fail as well, thereby reducing the unrealistic societal pressure for perfection. We are also perceived as human, real, and not untouchable. This simple act of admitting failure demonstrates a level of authenticity that not much else will achieve. As you make mistakes, admit them, but most importantly, learn from them, so you don't make them again. However, do not be ashamed to share your failures with others. It is liberating and authentic and will build connections with people.

The fear most leaders have about admitting failure is that they will be perceived as weak or incompetent. I've actually found the opposite to be true. When I have admitted mistakes and worked hard to correct them and learn from them, I have felt a greater sense of connection with people. Ultimately, as leaders that is what we are seeking, a genuine connection with people that allows us to influence them. I have realised in life that people will always have a perception of you. Sometimes it is true, other times not, but when you have rapport in place the false perceptions often dissipate as people have an authentic connection with you and understand your intentions regardless of your failures.

As a young leader I was overly sensitive to people's perceptions of me, and so I wanted everything to be perfect. I felt I needed to prove myself every day through being highly efficient and organised. I needed to be the perfect leader who everybody loved. Over time though, I have realised that the most important aspect of a leader's job is the ability to connect with people. This is where my priority should have been in those early years. Instead it was caught up in trying to make everything perfect so that I would be seen as a good leader and someone who was very efficient at his job. Chasing success and perfection is admirable, but I realised that my relentless pursuit of the unattainable was causing me to not be authentic with those I worked with. I was missing the connections. My approach was tiring and nearly led to me burning out. Of course, things need to function efficiently, but if your focus is controlled, like mine was, by the need to look good then you are sure to fail as this is not authentic. I hated making mistakes and would do everything I could to cover them up and not admit them. This was the picture of a perfect leader the world had created in my head.

As I developed as a leader I realised that failure is inevitable. We need to work efficiently and diligently to avoid it, but ultimately it will happen from time to time. When it did happen I began to share it with those around me and it was liberating. I had established rapport with my colleagues, which meant they were more forgiving than if I had not built a connection. They knew who I was as a leader and as a person, and therefore the mistakes I made did not lead to a breakdown in relationship or morale. Nowadays I admit my failures freely and regularly. It shows people that I am human and always willing to learn. Making mistakes is not bad. Not learning from them and repeating the same ones is the problem.

I reiterate that we should be avoiding mistakes at all cost in our lives, striving for efficiency and productivity. But failures will come, and when they do we should not be ashamed of them. Share your failures with your colleagues and let them know what you have done to rectify them. This freedom to share will breathe life into your office or team, who so often are risk averse due to the paralysing fear of failure. These small actions will demonstrate your authenticity to those around you.

Take a few minutes to reflect on the following questions before we move on to the next chapter.

1. What was the last mistake you made that impacted people around you?
2. How did this mistake make you feel?
3. What did you do to correct the mistake?
4. Did you share this failure with anyone?

The next time you make a mistake I encourage you to share the experience with someone immediately. As you begin to share your failures with those around you, you will notice a greater openness and connection with them. Sharing your failures demonstrates authenticity and authenticity builds rapport.

Professional Perspective
- Sheldon Kidwell, Cape Town, South Africa

Many of us tend, in conversation, to get very quickly to the question, "So what work do you do?" This is a small moment which helps a person subconsciously define where you fit in according to their frame of reference. Unfortunately, what we *do* should never define us. Rather, knowing who we *are* gives basis to our identity formed from our thinking, behaviour and character. This is a big question many ask: what is my purpose?

In my line of work I have the privilege of interacting with many people on a daily basis, and I am convinced more than ever that when a person truly knows their purpose, they are then able to authentically connect with other people. However, without the confidence that comes from knowing your purpose, building rapport is often forced and not sustainable.

Over time, our organisation has built a volunteer network of people who know their purpose and who display a genuine connection with one another. We witness this connection whenever our volunteers gather to serve in the various projects we have in place throughout our city, and this connection generates momentum for what we do. As a result, we place an exceptionally high priority on building rapport throughout our community as we see its value in our work every day.

Establishing and developing this network of people took time and required intentionality and consistency, and it wasn't without its challenges. However, as we diligently helped people discover their purpose in life, over time we found ourselves forming deep connections and relationships with people from all corners of our city. In my opinion this is the definition of rapport, people authentically connecting with each other regardless of their background or status.

Building rapport starts with knowing your purpose.

Sheldon Kidwell
Senior Pastor
Bay City Church

CHAPTER EIGHT

STRATEGY FOUR: CONSISTENCY

"For changes to be of any value, they have to be lasting and consistent." Tony Robbins

Consistency is the fourth strategic approach we will look at as a skill to develop in order to build rapport. I can't emphasise enough the importance of consistency and the effect it has on those around us. The reason I feel so strongly about consistency is that I believe it is the one thing that separates the good from the great. Whether it is being consistent in your interactions, work life, exercise, relationships or any other area of life, being consistent is the difference between achieving *good* outcomes or *great* outcomes. So whatever the context, consistency is always characterised by commitment and intent, and both of these characteristics are the very elements that will lead to success in any area of life. Think for a minute about a successful person that you know or admire. It can be success in any form not only financial success. I bet that the person you are thinking about embodies consistency in what they do. I do not know one person who I would deem successful who is not consistent in what they do. Success requires consistency, simple.

Earlier in the book we looked at emotional intelligence and how the ability to regulate your emotions consistently leads to success in building connections. Let us now look at consistency and why it is so key to positive and trustworthy interactions. One important fact is that when there is a lack of consistency a person's uncertainty levels rise. This is not good for rapport, as you need to instil certainty and trust with the other person as soon as possible. Without this there will be no rapport.

Being consistent means that regardless of emotional influences your interactions, demeanour and level of engagement with people remains the same. Your actions and interactions are not a roller-coaster ride in which people hope to catch you when it is going up, but avoid you when it is going down. If you are emotionally consistent, people will not notice an emotional spike or depression in your interactions and this consistency creates certainty and trust. Don't get me wrong, being authentic in displaying your emotions is important. We all have good days and bad days. If we didn't have them people would question our authenticity. However, even with the emotions attached to good and bad days, our interactions with others, and the way we approach our responsibilities should be consistent, not swinging from pillar to post by our emotions.

Think about rapport like a sieve which requires constant refilling. It is not a bucket that will remain full forever. Human connections require work, daily and consistently, in order to remain relevant and connected. That's why when you are building rapport with a person it is more about the small daily interactions you have with them, than one major event. Imagine everyone you work with carries a sieve around with them. Every day pour a little into each person's sieve, and if you do this consistently and daily you will see great results. What you don't want to do is take out the fire hydrant once a month and drench people, and then forget about them until the next month rolls around. Slow and steady wins the rapport race, without a doubt. Consistency is key.

Think about someone you know who you have to "walk on eggshells" around. It may be a family member, colleague or boss, but you'll know straight away who I'm talking about. You feel tentative and uneasy around them because they lack consistency. You never know what their reaction or response will be. Your uncertainty levels are sky high when interacting with them and more than likely, you lack trust in this person. An inconsistent person is incredibly hard to work with and often because of their inconsistency, they jump from job to job. In each position they find themselves in they are unable to establish authentic human connections — rapport. Often these people's lives are characterised by unending drama and issues. Do any people you know come to mind? Well, the feelings you have around these people are the exact feelings your colleagues will experience if you are inconsistent with them. The uncertainty and lack of trust you feel is not a feeling or experience you want to place on those around you

If you truly have a desire to build meaningful connections with people around you, you have to be emotionally, mentally and socially consistent. Let's take a deeper look into what consistency looks like in each of these three areas.

Mental Consistency

Mental consistency is when one's mental response to a situation or event remains constant, regardless of influences. For example, if you are in a position where you are required to make complex decisions regularly, you can demonstrate mental or cognitive consistency by ensuring that the outcome of your decisions are consistent and measured. People will then become accustomed to your decisions and their results, and will develop trust in you and your ability to perform. A mentally inconsistent person uses their mental capacity to make cognitive decisions, but the outcomes are erratic. People do not know what to expect from them and as a result do not trust their decisions as the outcome is inconsistent. It is therefore important that the decisions you make result in a consistent outcome, which people can then trust. While the context may change from decision to decision, and even your approach, if people trust that your involvement usually leads to a relied upon result, you will be viewed as mentally consistent. Mental consistency is especially important to those in leadership positions who are required to make daily decisions.

When someone makes consistent decisions that are dependable and effective, they will be trusted. The ability to make highly effective decisions consistently comes largely through experience, but it is also a skill which can be developed intentionally. I make it my goal in every organisation I work in to observe the decision-makers and the outcome of their decisions. By doing this I learn from their successes and failures in addition to learning from my experiences. I believe a person can bypass the need for personal experience by actively seeking out experienced decision-makers and then learning alongside them. In all honesty, I learn more from the poor decisions and failures I see around me than I do from the successes. This relates to the previous chapter on celebrating failure, and reminds me of the importance of admitting failure and learning from it. Approach your decision-making process methodically and consistently and you will very quickly gain the trust of those around you. Rash or erratic decisions will quickly lead to a loss of credibility and dependability and will limit rapport.

Emotional Consistency

The ability to remain emotionally consistent regardless of the circumstance is essential when building rapport. People lack trust in emotionally inconsistent people as they are not certain of their emotional state or response at any given time. The term "walking on eggshells" is a great way to describe how people feel when interacting with an emotionally inconsistent person. Saying the wrong thing or acting in the wrong way can lead to an irrational reaction. No one enjoys being in the presence of these people. However, emotional consistency allows one to rise above the inevitable daily emotional fluctuations and portray a consistent emotional state through one's actions.

There are many reasons that could lead to a person being emotionally inconsistent, but through the process of reflection they can gain awareness of their emotional state and then develop the ability to regulate their emotions accordingly. Once someone has control of their emotions, this incredibly powerful aspect of being human, they can then act in a consistent manner through the process of regulation. When a person does not have an awareness of their emotions and is not able to regulate them effectively, their daily actions and interactions will be influenced by their emotional state. Like a rudderless ship they are at the mercy of whatever emotional wind blows. Awareness is the foundation of regulation and without the ability to regulate emotions a person will always have the tendency to be inconsistent in their interactions.

If you are viewed by those around you as an emotionally consistent person, then you have the ability to step outside the immediate situation you are faced with, gain an awareness of your emotional state and regulate it accordingly through your actions. This can be done in a moment and will bring about consistency in your emotions and their influence on your body. Continue to practice the reflection exercises already discussed in this book to gain control of your emotions. This will result in an increased emotional consistency, which in turn will result in deeper rapport with those around you.

Social Consistency

Social consistency is the ability to demonstrate consistency in your interactions, friendships and connections with others. As you interact with people over time you will be viewed as either socially consistent or inconsistent due to your actions, responses and demeanour. People won't necessarily use these words, but they will place you in a certain box according to their experience with you. People who are generally easy-going and authentic will be viewed as having a higher social consistency, which is appealing to people. Those who struggle with being open and honest with others and who are emotionally demanding will struggle to build deep connections, and therefore will exhibit a level of inconsistency socially. If people do not know what to expect from you then obviously you will be seen as inconsistent. But if people are confident to approach you, if they have a high level of certainty in you, it is because you are consistent. People will avoid interacting with you if your response to their needs is usually inconsistent or varied. Rather, people are attracted to socially consistent people as there is certainty and generally a high degree of trust as they interact.

It is important that you strive for consistency in these three areas of your life as they will dramatically impact the level of rapport you can build with people. The inability to regulate your emotions consistently will lead to erratic responses as you interact with people. Therefore, work diligently on gaining an awareness of your emotions and how your emotions influence your body. With this understanding and awareness you will be able to regulate your actions and responses while interacting with people. This level of emotional understanding and control will lead to consistency. Let's move on to another reflection exercise to help with this.

Reflection Exercise

I have said it before; awareness is the foundation of regulation. Regulating all of your consistency levels begins with gaining an awareness of your current mental, emotional and social consistency level. However, you cannot come to this awareness alone. You need an external, objective perspective. Take some time to follow this three-step exercise in order to reflect on your current level of consistency in your daily interactions.

Step One:

Carefully select five people who you can approach to help you in this area. You need to be very selective in order to get a true reflection of yourself. I encourage you to select people you interact with every few days. Ideally you do not want them to be a close friend or someone you would spend time with socially. They need to have regular interactions with you, but cannot be so close that they feel pressured to tell you what you want to hear. If you are selecting people from your work, choose those who are on the same employee level as you or higher. Choosing a person who reports to you won't lead to an accurate result. Go ahead and write five names down.

Step Two:

Once you have carefully selected five people, give them a brief introduction of your intentions and let them know that you value their honest opinion. Then, ask each of them the following questions:

1. Do you feel that I approach all of our interactions in a consistent manner?
2. Do you have confidence in the decisions I make?
3. Do you ever notice spikes in my emotions?
4. Do you ever feel hesitant to approach me? If so, why?

Step Three:

Once you have received the feedback, it is critical that you evaluate it from an impartial perspective. If you have chosen well, you should have received very valuable feedback to the four simple questions. These four questions are designed to give you an awareness of your mental, emotional and social consistency, although it is quite hard to separate each of these areas as they are so interconnected. The most important question is number four as this will paint an overall picture of your approachability. Ultimately, consistency is one of the main tenets of approachability. While there may be other factors, if people feel confident that they can approach you then you are generally viewed by most as consistent.

If people answer your questions negatively, in particular question three and four, then you need to critically evaluate your level of consistency during interactions. This is a red flag that needs to be acknowledged as rapport is severely limited by inconsistency. Use the exercises outlined in previous chapters to regulate your emotions and begin to control them for your benefit. As your emotional awareness increases, so too will your ability to regulate your emotions, and this will result in you being more emotionally consistent.

If you get a negative response to question four, ask the person for further insights as to why they feel hesitant to approach you. Listen humbly without trying to justify your position. The chances are if one person is feeling hesitant to approach you, others are too. Take stock of your social interactions by hearing this feedback, and then create an action plan where you can work on being more consistent in your dealings with people. Some changes might be small habits that you need to get rid of, others may be more complex. The important thing is to identify them and then work to eradicate them. As you do this your approachability will increase and so too your ability to build rapport. It is important to continually revisit this process until the feedback you receive is in line with your objectives.

The Forest Man of India

With the understanding of the importance of consistency, I would like to share a story with you. The story typifies consistency and what our approach with people should look like. As I read this story I am reminded that consistency, in all forms, is not reliant on money or social status. It is an attitude and understanding that is intentionally demonstrated through one's actions. Let me introduce you to Jadav Payeng.

Jadav grew up in a very poor family in India, the third of 13 children whose parents sold milk from their herd of cattle to earn a living. At the age of five due to extreme poverty, his family had no choice but to leave him with another family in the community, who oversaw his schooling. However, when his parents passed away this forced him to leave school uncompleted in order to tend to the family herd, so that he could support his family.

It was in 1979, after intense flooding of the Brahmaputra River, that Jadav was struck by the vast amount of small animals washed away by the waters onto the uninhabitable and hostile floodplains – they were all left dead as the water retreated. He was only a young teenager at the time, but knew that the absence of vegetation was exacerbating land erosion and endangering animals and humans on Majuli Island where he lived. Actually, when he was a child his entire village had been washed away and this had a profound impact on him growing up. He realised that the world's largest river island was being slowly eroded by the river.

He decided then that he wanted to do something to save Majuli. After speaking with the elders in the community, who didn't share his enthusiasm, he began planting bamboo on one of Majuli's constantly eroding river banks. His original idea came from a government forestation project he began working on the same year, located a few kilometres away, which planted 2 square kilometres of trees over five years. It was during this project that Jadav learned the proper techniques for sowing seeds, and of the various tree and plant species that would thrive in the hostile environment of sand, silt and flooding. He helped complete the government project and even opted to stay on after everyone else had left to care for the saplings, while also making time to plant trees every day on Majuli.

He asked the government for help in reforesting Majuli on numerous occasions. However, they declined. So without becoming disheartened, and working on his own, Jadav planted new seeds as well as tended to the original bamboo every day, while also adding additional plants and different varieties of trees.

It was a massive commitment, involving a relentless daily search for seeds, saplings and fertiliser, while also identifying insects such as red ants to introduce to the area to improve the ecosystem. All of these efforts represented a significant financial sacrifice, since he used the minimal income from his milk sales to fund the environmental rebirth of this island. After five years of hard work, he had spanned one kilometre, which was gradually covered by dense vegetation. Over the years, the members of the community began to call him 'Molai', meaning 'forest', and called his woodland *Molai Forest*.

Jadav never stopped planting. Even in 2011, after he moved away from Majuli to be closer to schools and services for his children, he continued to grow the forest while still caring for his family's herd and selling milk. Nowadays he wakes at 3am, cycles for an hour, rows a boat for about five kilometres, and then cycles again for 30 more minutes to reach his families' original farm. After he arrives he milks the cows and collects manure which he uses for fertiliser. By 9am, he is then able to focus on his forest.

It is nearly four decades since Jadav started planting seeds on Majuli and it now covers some 5.6 square kilometres, nearly twice the size of New York's Central Park. Thanks to his consistent efforts, the island of Majuli did not erode away as had been feared and the community was revitalised.

In addition to his focus on forest expansion, Jadav's goals have extended to include conservation and wildlife protection as well. These days, his forest is home to endangered Bengal tigers, one-horned rhinos, exotic birds and over a hundred wild boar and deer. There is also a herd of around 100 elephants that migrate there every year for several months, not to mention the wide range of small animals and insects that form a healthy ecosystem.

Considering the wide range of animal life, new threats to the ecosystem have arisen. Therefore, Jadav has become highly active in helping to catch poachers in the area, and in protecting the forest from the ever expanding human population. He is now a renowned conservationist in the area and regularly speaks at environmental gatherings. Considering his experience, he believes in identifying community-based solutions to environmental destruction and poaching, rather than relying on government support.

At the age of 54, Jadav is continuing to identify desolate and infertile land on which to start planting – with the goal of covering another 20 square kilometres with forest. He has also turned to educating others and hopes that his achievements will inspire them to take action in caring for the environment. Jadav believes passionately in his cause and says "*In India, every child has to learn environmental science. Education should be changed in such a way that each child should plant two trees, thus earning their own oxygen. If a child plants a tree, they will not let anyone cut it down. They will not let anyone harm the birds. They will not let anyone harm the animals. We must implement this in India and all over the world."*

He believes that this will have a significant impact in saving the world from the negative effects of climate change. *"There will be no more global warming if everyone plants forests,"* he says.

While Jadav's story is overwhelmingly inspiring, it is also an amazing example of consistency. His consistent approach, driven by a passion for the natural world around him, led to him establishing something sustainable and beneficial to his community and the region. From this story you can learn to approach everyone you interact with as your natural environment, and as you consistently plant positive seeds in their lives, over time they will yield an amazing harvest.

Remember, rapport is not developed through a once-off event, rather it is built through the regular and consistent daily interactions you have with people. When your interactions with people are positive and consistently focused on their best interests, over time you will establish strong and authentic rapport with them.

Professional Perspective
- Dorothy Raine, Cape Town, South Africa

"Education is the most powerful weapon which you can use to change the world." - Nelson Mandela

Having been a teacher and administrator in a variety of schools for many years, I can reflect on what it took to develop an environment for effective teaching, learning and positive growth to occur. I believe that the biggest factor in academic success is the relationship between the teacher and the student.

Regardless of context, whenever I have observed a highly engaged and connected teacher, I have seen students academically progress significantly more than when there is no connection evident. Often, the rapport in the classroom, staffroom or parent meetings develops quite easily and naturally, while at other times intentional strategies are needed to develop a meaningful rapport in a situation.

Since retiring, I have been working for a trust whose vision is "to turn public schools serving socio-economically disadvantaged communities into centres of excellence and beacons of hope." I am involved with the Teacher Support Programme run by the trust.

So, whether working in a very affluent community or with the most disadvantaged of society I have found that in most cases we all respond positively when we feel accepted, acknowledged and affirmed as individuals. In order to develop authentic communication and good rapport the basic needs and psychological needs of all humans must be met with genuine empathy, respect and love.

As a leader of a group, chairman of a meeting or presenter in a workshop the importance of humility cannot be over emphasised. Nothing kills rapport more than one-upmanship or superiority on the part of the leader.

Dorothy Raine
The Principals Academy

Chapter Nine

Strategy Five: Energy and Enthusiasm

"Enthusiasm, if fuelled by inspiration and perseverance,
travels with passion and its destination is excellence."
Napoleon Hill

The world is made up of two kinds of people, those that build energy and those that take energy. Every human being on the face of this earth can be placed into one of these two categories. And yes, one person can be both an energy-builder and an energy-taker at various points in their life depending on their circumstances. Reflect for a minute about those people you interact with on a daily or weekly basis. I'm sure you can fairly quickly identify an energy-taker or energy vampire as I often call them. They are the ones who quite literally drain all of your energy through negativity or emotional neediness, requiring constant attention.

On the other hand, I'm sure you can quickly identify an energy-builder you interact with regularly. Energy-builders are people who leave you feeling positive, energised and enthusiastic after an interaction. These people are like gold to an organisation and need to be treasured as they have the ability to shift the energy in a room simply through their presence. The reality though is that many companies lack these vital energy-builders and find themselves stuck with energy-takers who require constant attention and support. I've observed that an energy-builder will not remain in an organisation long term unless there are other like-minded energy-builders to work alongside, as there is nothing that frustrates energy-builders more than energy-takers.

Energy-takers have the potential to drain the energy and enthusiasm out of even the strongest energy-builder. So often, energy-builders avoid energy-takers altogether. Energy-takers on the other hand tend to be more complacent and if not challenged will remain stagnant in an organisation, often irrespective of the people around them. I've noticed that energy-takers tend to swarm together in organisations and this can often lead to a negative or toxic culture creeping in. Energy-takers are exposed when around energy-builders and so will not voluntarily associate with them.

During my time in leadership I have experienced both energy takers and energy builders and this has caused me to reflect on what I bring to a room full of people or an organisation. Am I an energy-builder, or am I an energy vampire? This is an important question that we need to regularly ask ourselves. I try my best to be intentional about being an energy-builder because I see the value this brings to people. I don't get it right every time, but I am intentional about it. When you are intentional about something, over time it becomes a default action. As a leader, I have made a conscious effort to invest the majority of my time in energy-builders. They are the people driving the organisation, who are building connections, and who are ambitious about their futures. Their positive disposition is contagious and they need to be encouraged. While I don't completely neglect the energy-takers, I am aware that often, regardless of what I do, their opinion and disposition never changes. Therefore, I choose to invest my time in people in whom I can see growth and potential.

An energy-taker is often that way due to circumstances in their personal life, seldom due to their experience at work. People more often than not bring baggage from home to their work environment, not the other way around. Therefore, when I come across an energy-taker, I know that there is often something in their personal life which is causing their behaviour. An employee's home life will significantly affect their performance at work and will dictate whether they become an energy-builder or taker.

This is the reason why building connections that span beyond the work environment is so critical.

Being aware of whether you are an energy-builder or energy-taker is very important as your ability to develop authentic rapport is closely linked to this status. While energy-takers can absolutely build rapport with others, they tend to only build rapport with fellow energy-takers. Their commonalities are often gossip, negativity or complaining. Energy-builders, on the other hand, are able to build rapport with everyone as people are drawn to them due to their ability to inspire, motivate and encourage. Simply put, energy-builders choose to focus on the positive, while energy-takers regularly choose to focus on the negative.

Managing your energy and enthusiasm levels stems directly from your mindset. People with a positive outlook on the world and a growth mindset will naturally have higher enthusiasm and energy levels. This is because your physical actions are a byproduct of your mental and emotional state. Have you ever noticed your energy and enthusiasm levels when you are having a bad day or you are struggling with something? They will be a lot lower. No one is immune to this; we all have good days and bad days. However, the ability to regulate our emotions so that even when we are having a bad day our outlook remains positive is the key. Positivity is a choice which needs to be made every morning. I'm a big believer in this and I have seen the impact of choosing positivity in my daily life. I find it easier to choose to be positive after I consider how blessed I am. Actually, reflecting on my life and gaining perspective on how blessed I am is part of my morning routine.

When I consider the amount of suffering and tragedy there is in the world, I am reminded that the struggles I face pale in comparison. A brief reflection on the positive things in your life will quickly result in a positive mindset for the day. In the previous chapter you read about consistency. Well, this is equally important when it comes to your energy levels and enthusiasm. People should see a constant level of energy and enthusiasm coming from you regardless of your emotional state. This is the goal of regulating your emotions, the ability to remain constant irrespective of external influences in your life. So on those days when things aren't going your way, the ability to regulate your emotions will reduce the fluctuations people see in your energy and enthusiasm levels.

Energy-builders and energy-takers are not just building or taking physical energy. They are influencing someone's emotional energy as well. Everyone has an emotional energy reserve, kind of like a petrol tank in a car. Some people have a large reserve, while others a smaller one. When this reserve runs dry their emotional state changes and can be displayed in moods, anger, anxiety, and frustration. On the other hand, when this emotional energy reserve overflows it is displayed in laughter, joy, fulfilment, and excitement. Gauging a person's emotional energy reserves is an important skill, which can be acquired through rapport. I often only need to observe or listen to a person I have rapport with in order to gauge if their emotional reserves are high or low. This then informs the way I interact with them. Essentially, this is emotional intelligence at work.

This is why being an energy-builder is so important for building rapport. It relates directly to our emotional energy levels, which impact every area of a person's life. Building emotional energy in people is what has a lasting impact. Physical energy is definitely important as well, as our emotions and physicality are interconnected. Therefore, it is vital that in your desire to build rapport you become a regular energy-builder, someone people want to be around. Energy and enthusiasm are contagious, and the more you display them, together with positive affirmations, the more you will build authentic connections. People are drawn to energy-builders and enthusiastic people, whereas people more often than not choose to avoid energy-takers. Be an energy-builder!

As you strive to be an energy-builder, it is important that you never lose authenticity. It is obvious when someone is trying to be positive, happy and enthusiastic, when they actually are not. It's quite awkward. It has to be authentic. You genuinely need to have a desire to build energy in people and positively influence them. This is the defining characteristic.

So how does one become an energy-builder, someone who through enthusiasm can uplift the emotional energy reserves of others? Believe it or not, only a small percentage has to do with your physical energy levels; a lot more has to do with your emotional energy levels. However, it definitely requires physical energy. You need to move and talk in such a way that you display positive, physical energy. These actions will together set the tone for the transfer of energy from you to the other person. But in addition to your display of physical energy, you become an energy-builder by building emotional capital within people. In other words, by filling up their emotional energy reserves. There is one simple word for this — encouragement.

As you encourage people, as you become their number one cheerleader, you will build their emotional energy reserves. The most effective way to become an energy-builder is to focus on all the good that people are doing, and encourage them in that. Let them know that you are there for them, supporting them and most importantly, believing in them. This form of encouragement is rare in many organisations, yet is one of the most effective ways to build rapport. Working in education I have noticed that towards the end of an academic year teachers tend to be emotionally depleted as their emotional energy reserves are at rock bottom. This is understandable as teaching is such an emotionally draining profession. If you don't believe me go ahead and teach a class of children for the day and let me know how you feel afterwards. As a teacher you are invested in so much more than a job, you are emotionally invested in the lives of your students and there is a burden that accompanies this. Anyway, as I was saying, towards the end of the academic year I know that teachers are emotionally low and their actions tend to reflect their emotional depletion. As a leader in this context, while I may be feeling equally drained, it is the perfect opportunity to build people's emotional energy levels through encouragement. It is also important to remember that during these times of emotional depletion, teachers will respond differently compared to when their emotional energy tanks are overflowing. Either way, and in every situation, encouragement will increase emotional energy levels and might be just what someone needs to get them over the finish line.

An energy-taker generally criticises a lot, which is the complete opposite to an energy-builder who provides a consistent stream of encouragement to those around them. Regardless of what the outcome is, I choose to show authentic encouragement for the effort and commitment I see in people. By choosing to value and praise the *process* and not always the *product* you will find countless opportunities to encourage people. If you are fixated on the outcome of a particular project, and it fails, you won't have an opportunity to show praise. Actually, your demeanour might lead to discouragement in the person.

So, are you currently an energy-taker or energy-builder? You can gain an awareness of this quite easily by reflecting on how much time you spend criticising and complaining compared to how much time you spend encouraging and praising those around you. If you want another opinion, ask someone who is not one of your colleagues or a close friend to get an accurate perspective. Reflecting on their feedback is really important and should always lead to action. Being an energy-builder is a choice a person makes every morning. So, be intentional about building emotional energy in those around you today.

The world needs more energy-builders. This intentional action requires practice and dedication to become part of your daily habits. If it helps, make a daily list of the people you want to encourage, and then reflect at the end of the day on whether you achieved your objective. This should be done in conjunction with the authentic, spontaneous encouragement you provide people as you interact with them.

Richard Branson, one of the world's most respected entrepreneurs, says, *"Lavish praise on people and people will flourish, criticise people and they'll shrivel up."* By being an energy-builder you are positively influencing a person beyond their needs at work, impacting other areas of their lives too. This approach, when authentic, will lead to a deep human connection.

CHAPTER TEN

STRATEGY SIX: INTENTIONALITY

"Wanting to win isn't enough. You have to go through a process to improve. That takes patience, perseverance and intentionality." John C. Maxwell

Some people have the natural ability to build authentic emotional connections with people without trying very hard. It is a skill they have acquired over time without actually noticing it. Whether it was through their family upbringing, relationships, and mentoring while at work, or simply through a God-given talent, they bring out the best in others. Their natural thoughts and actions lend themselves to the strategies mentioned in this book, and it is not a process they need to consciously develop. However, whether building rapport comes naturally to you or not, I highly recommend being intentional about developing further relational strategies and skills. There is always room for growth. It is dangerous to think we have fully mastered a certain ability or skill. That is when complacency creeps in.

But for others, building rapport doesn't come naturally. It requires intentional action until it becomes second nature. There could be a range of factors that make building connections with others difficult. For these people the process requires dedication and commitment. However, I have every confidence that everyone, regardless of background, can develop the skills required to authentically connect with others.

Ultimately, the desire for human connection is deep within all of us. It just requires unlocking.

Building rapport is a skill that requires intentional action. It requires people to direct their thinking and actions towards establishing an authentic emotional connection with other people. Some people will require more intentionality than others. However, one cannot simply remain passive and expect rapport to be developed without intention. It requires action executed consistently in order to have a lasting impact. Being intentional is a strategy that is not often used when it comes to building rapport. I regularly hear it said that some people have a 'relational ability' while others don't. While I agree that some people have a higher emotional intelligence and therefore perceive other people's feelings and emotional states better than others, I believe that everyone has the ability to connect with others. Connection is one of our most fundamental needs as human beings. The difference is that some people are intentional about building connections while others aren't. It comes down to how much value you place on it. Like anything in life, if a person places value on it they will be intentional about chasing after it. How much value do you place on rapport?

There is a perception that if you are not labelled as 'relational' then building rapport is not for you. You are somehow exempt from making an effort with people. However, this thinking is completely flawed. Every human being is relational as we are driven to a large extent by our emotions and the connections we establish with those around us. Therefore, everyone needs to be intentional about building rapport. Unfortunately, this tends to be a blind spot for many.

As I grew up I developed a passion for sport, which continues to this day. While I did have my favourite sports, I was generally happy playing any sport. However, as I moved through high school and on to university it became evident that if I was going to succeed I would need to be intentional about training, eating and practising consistently. The level of intentionality I required to be successful in sport during middle and high school fell well short of what was required in university. All of a sudden I was competing against a lot more players, many of whom were exceptional athletes. I had to be focused on my objectives and work hard to achieve them. The success I enjoyed in high school was not going to be replicated in university unless I put more effort in.

In the same way, some people can build rapport by just being themselves. They have an increased relational ability and emotional intelligence that allows them to connect easily with others. However, being unintentional about building rapport will have the same success as being unintentional about training for a big game. You may get lucky and get a few intercepts during the game, but you will never have consistent victories because your success is linked to the amount of work you put in. Being intentional about your daily interactions over time will lead to deep connections and rapport. Just like victory was always on my mind whenever I put on my rugby jersey, rapport should always be on yours when you consider your plans for the day. By starting your day this way you will be more intentional about how you interact with others.

There are countless examples of the greatest athletes in history continuing to put in more work than some of their younger and less experienced teammates. One would think that Michael Jordan, Sachin Tendulkar, Gary Player and Tom Brady earned the right to slack off a bit in their training and allow their experience and natural talent to carry them later in their careers. However, this was never the case and they continued to put hours of work in every day to chase success. Athletes at the top of their game are there due to their dedication to intentionality. Right up until that final match, they are intentional about being the best, dedicated to put in the work required to get them there.

The higher the value you place on rapport, the more intentional you will be about working on it. To this end you need to view rapport as a critical skill you cannot live without. Imagine if you were a very bad communicator and you were regularly told that this was an area of weakness in your professional life. You would be very intentional about developing the skills required to communicate better, as communication is such a vital skill for most professions. I'm sure you would get public speaking training and perhaps even find a mentor who could coach you to improve in this skill. So why don't people approach rapport with the same urgency as we do other professional skills? I believe there are two reasons. Firstly, I do not believe people truly understand the positive impact rapport has in a professional setting; and secondly, measuring rapport is not as clear-cut as measuring other more linear areas at work. Measuring the impact of rapport is a qualitative measurement as opposed to a more specific quantitative measurement like we find in a sales process.

When you truly understand that rapport is as important as communication, decision-making and executing your daily expectations, you will place a higher priority on intentionally developing the required skills. Being intentional about building rapport is essential to success and needs to be viewed as being as critical as other skills such as communication, collaboration and execution of tasks.

Daily Intentionality

Doing small things every day to build a genuine emotional connection with people always outweighs a once-off big event. Thankfully, I am one of those people who find it very easy to connect with people; in fact, I really enjoy it. However, over time I have realised that to make a lasting impact I also need to be intentional about building rapport. I cannot simply sit back and trust that my natural demeanour is good enough. It isn't. It requires work and intentionality to be effective and long-lasting.

Every day I set myself a goal of positively impacting those around me. This is a very conscious and intentional start to my day. Sometimes this impact is in the form of an encouraging email, or better still, a handwritten note. Other times I make the effort to go and see people who I haven't connected with in a while. I purposely initiate a brief conversation to check in with the other person, evaluate their energy reserves and encourage them. My goal for these brief interactions is to leave them in a more positive frame of mind than before. The reason for these brief face-to-face interactions is simply to keep the momentum of rapport between us flowing. Remember that humans are like sieves when it comes to rapport — we need regular filling. Just because you have a connection with someone in place doesn't mean you stop making the effort. Consistent and intentional effort is required to build sustainable rapport, and for me this means regular interactions and touchpoints.

While I don't write down a specific goal or human 'target' for each day, I do know people who do and it works for them. They select two or three people each day who they are intentional about connecting with, in addition to the inevitable interactions they will have with other people throughout the day. This strategy is often used until intentionality becomes habitual. Often the human brain requires a few weeks of manual stimulation before automation kicks in through learned and repeated behaviour. I do not set a human 'target' each day, but I do reflect on who I haven't connected with recently and I am intentional about interacting with them during the day. Other than that, I am always on the lookout for opportunities to connect with people, both formally and informally.

Being intentional about building rapport every day is about being aware of where people are at emotionally and personally. I make a point of remembering things people say to me so that the next time I see them there is a natural continuation of the emotional connection. For example, remembering people's children's names, recent successes or tragedies in their families, or previous experiences they have gone through, all demonstrate empathy. It is often the small details that leave the biggest impression on a person, and it requires intentionality to develop the skills to remember and recall things people share. As you end your conversation with someone, call to mind what they have shared with you and make a mental, or physical, note that will help you recall this information the next time you meet. Once again, this may come naturally to you. If it does, use this ability to recall important information to re-establish an emotional connection the next time you meet them. If you struggle to recall important information people share with you, be intentional about remembering the details of your conversation. As you are intentional about remembering important personal information, you will see an increase in your ability to recall it in your future meetings.

It is all about being intentional — no skill is acquired or developed without work. Underpinning all of these strategies must be a genuine interest in the person you are building rapport with. I cannot state this enough. In all of my intentions to build rapport, I have a genuine interest in the other person's well-being. This is so important as rapport is nothing if it is not authentic. It's worth saying at this point too, that I make mistakes every day and am by no means a perfect person. I get relationships wrong at times and I unintentionally offend people. However, I understand the value of rapport and so I continue to be intentional about building it regardless of when I mess up. Don't be discouraged if you mess up. Keep pressing on by being intentional.

In my current line of work as a school administrator, I could very easily find myself trapped in my office from 8 to 5 every day. The workload is seemingly never-ending and the problems to resolve keep coming. However, I try to be intentional about getting out of my office several times during the day to just interact with our staff and students without an agenda. Not only is this good leadership practice, but it is vital within the context of a school where so many stakeholders influence daily decisions. Having a presence around our school campus is reassuring to staff and students, and provides wonderful opportunities for brief positive interactions and encouragement. It is not always possible to get out of the office, that's just the reality, but unless I am intentional about doing so the days simply whizz by. Rapport, like most areas of leadership, cannot be built from behind a desk. Be intentional about meeting people where they are, both physically and emotionally.

One strategy I use to help me prioritise building rapport is to block time in my calendar every day for human connections. By being intentional about this I can ensure that I have a minimum amount of time where I am interacting with others. That way, even during manic days I know I have time set aside devoted to connecting with others. As these times are locked into my calendar, which is shared with everyone in the organisation, I know I won't be drawn into meetings, interviews or other tasks during these times. I fight hard to protect these times of connecting as I value rapport as highly as any other professional skill. Being intentional with your time is so important, and finding a strategy to help you manage the time in your day will be beneficial. The problem with not being intentional about building rapport is that it is always seen as an afterthought, something you'll get to "when you have time". The reality is that in most professions there is never enough time. Intentionality in developing this skill is critical. Rapport will not build itself.

Regardless of whether building rapport comes naturally to you or not, you need to be intentional about building and fostering human connections with people. Set time aside every day when you can be intentional about connecting with people. I also encourage you to keep a note, either literally or in your head, of who you have and haven't connected with. This simple strategy will help you to build rapport consistently across your workplace, as opposed to only with the select few with whom you share an obvious bond or connection.

Intuition

> *"If you can make a decision with analysis, you should do so. But it turns out in life that your most important decisions are always made with instinct and intuition."* - Jeff Bezos, technology entrepreneur and founder of Amazon.

Intuition is the built-in ability we all have to intuitively and instinctively understand a situation or experience. It is often referred to as one's 'gut feel' because it is not driven by conscious reasoning, but rather through an emotional feeling one experiences. Intuition is a vital component of rapport as it links directly with a person's emotions. As discussed throughout this book, a connection with your own emotions is critical to understanding and empathising with the emotional state of others. A large part of building rapport is driven by the feeling you receive when interacting with others and not always the obvious signs in front of you. Therefore, it is important to understand intuition and develop your ability to hear and feel your inner voice.

Humans do not have varying degrees of intuition. I believe we all have this attribute in equal measure. However, people have varying abilities of listening and responding to their intuition. Being led by your intuition is a skill that requires development. The more you are able to 'feel' your intuition and be led by it, the louder that inner voice will become. If you constantly rely on conscious reasoning your intuition will not diminish. However, your ability to hear it, feel it and act upon it will not be as prevalent. This is where our emotions become a powerful tool in the decision-making process, as our emotions perceive things that our cognitive reasoning does not.

For example, I rely heavily on my intuition when interviewing potential staff. I am intentional during these interviews to allow time to 'feel' who the candidate really is and what they can bring to our organisation. Most candidates who make it through our recruitment filtering and reach the stage of an interview are cognitively strong with years of experience. Therefore, I am confident they could execute their daily responsibilities as expected. However, during the interview I am more concerned with how they will connect with other staff members, how they will influence our organisational culture, and whether they are an energy-taker or energy-builder. I rely heavily on my intuition to guide me. Sure, it does come with experience, but it also comes through developing the ability to use it, by being intentional about accessing this powerful decision-making ability. Very seldom has my intuition about a candidate or decision been wrong.

Intuition is a vital part of the rapport-building process as emotions are at the centre of rapport. If a person lacks the ability to hear and feel their intuition, then they negate a large part of their ability to establish a connection with people. While conscious reasoning will always play a part in building rapport, it is largely overshadowed by a person's understanding of emotions and the role they play in people's lives.

Regardless of who you are or your work context, your intuition is speaking to you throughout the day. For many people, they are not aware of this due to the clutter and busyness of their daily lives. Therefore, in order to develop your ability to hear and feel your intuition and be led by it, it is important that you take time every day to acknowledge your inner voice. The more time you give to your intuition, the louder it will become.

Here is a five-step process I follow which allows my intuition time to help me make decisions in conjunction with my conscious reasoning.

When faced with a circumstance or a situation that requires action:

1. Pause. Allow time for your brain and intuition to process the context of the situation. Many times we are so quick to respond that we do not allow ourselves time to emotionally and cognitively process the situation or decision.
2. Ask yourself, "What is my intuition telling me?"
3. Pause. Allow yourself time to feel your intuition and what your emotions are telling you.
4. Develop a response which combines your intuition and conscious reasoning.
5. Act.

This simple five-step process can take place in a matter of seconds once a person has developed the skill of listening to their intuition. It may take a bit longer for a person still developing these skills, but over time it will become natural. The important thing is that you are intentional about listening to your intuition, and to not always responding with only conscious reasoning.

In addition to using your intuition during a decision-making process, whenever you interact with people ask yourself, "What is my intuition telling me about this person?" By allowing yourself to be led by your intuition you will be amazed at the connections you will make with people. Your intuition will tell you a lot more about what is happening in someone's life than your conscious reasoning will. As you develop the ability to hear and feel your intuition, and be guided by it, the process will become second nature to you and part of your daily experience.

I consider all of my interactions with people throughout the day to be opportunities to build rapport, and I have many examples of how my intuition has guided my conversations and actions. By no means am I an expert in this area. However, it is an area I believe in and therefore I create space for it in my daily interactions. By allowing your intuition time to guide you, you will be surprised at the insights you gain into the lives of people, as well as into the unseen complexities of certain situations. One of the reasons that I believe intuition is so powerful is that it often cuts away the superficial masks people sometimes put on. Intuition is the ultimate separator between the authentic and the superficial.

I remember holding an appraisal meeting with one of my previous staff members. The staff member was a highly efficient team member and regularly contributed to our organisation's success. So on the surface everything seemed to be going well and an image of success was created through this person's daily actions. However, as I was conducting this appraisal meeting, I felt that this person was facing personal challenges at work and needed support in a certain area. This was my intuition speaking to me in response to what the team member was sharing. As a result of following my intuition I was able to ask relevant questions and offer the solutions and support that were required. The meeting was highly successful and once again showed me the importance of creating space to hear your intuition and follow it. We both left the meeting with a new sense of connection and understanding, and I know without a doubt that listening to my intuition played a big role in that meeting's success.

I try to be led by my intuition throughout the day. This requires intentionality as our default thought pattern tends to be driven by our conscious reasoning. Our brains are so powerful and can provide solutions within an instant. However, we must realise that while these solutions often seem accurate, they are one-dimensional. Our cognitive function is vital and should never be downplayed, but the ability to hear our intuition and 'feel' a situation is one of the most powerful tools in building rapport.

Intent in Action

Intent is often a precursor to success as it is the ability to commit daily to a course of action that is linked to a dream or desire. Without it a person's aspirations will never be realised, as a consistent and focused approach is required in order to attain any goal. Intent is also the commitment to do something even when you don't feel like doing it. This is how people realise success, when they are intentional about achieving an outcome regardless of their physical, mental or emotional state. Intent is the ability to keep your eyes fixed on the goal and then consistently work towards achieving it. The Forest Man of India, Jadav, is a wonderful example of intent; day after day, consistently working towards an outcome. This commitment to achieve a desired outcome comes from a passion to see a goal realised. The more desire and passion a person has to achieve something, the more intent they will have, as it is their passion that carries them during the tough times.

Many talented athletes have failed to reach their potential because they lacked intent. They simply lacked the drive to consistently and intentionally train for a specific purpose. They may have been gifted with world-class talent, but talent will always be overtaken by hard work and desire. Demonstrating intent will lead to success in all areas of your life, not only in building rapport. It is a powerful attribute that you can use to achieve great things. When you are intentional about doing something, you are focused, and when you are focused your actions are aligned with your desires.

As you use the strategies in this book, be very intentional about how you go about building rapport with people. Focus on a few things that you can do consistently every day that will make a positive impact in people's lives. The small things, done consistently and intentionally, will yield great results.

Professional Perspective
- Neil White, Singapore

My name is Neil White, and I am a dedicated school administrator passionate about developing students' knowledge and experiences within a diverse, international learning environment. For the past 20 years I have worked in schools across the Middle East, the U.K. and South East Asia in a variety of both teaching and administrative roles.

Throughout my time in education, I have come to understand the value of positive relationships and the impact they have on all aspects of school life. Building rapport should be a highly valued concept within any organisation. The ways in which we engage and interact with others on a daily basis speaks volumes about who we are and what we value.

Rapport is the cornerstone for building trust and developing positive relationships. It doesn't just happen, it needs to be developed and maintained to build a positive culture. Through establishing rapport, employees feel valued and in turn, they are much more likely to express their needs and to contribute their thoughts and their ideas. They know that when they do this, it matters to you and to the organisation. This leads to improved satisfaction and effective productivity throughout the workplace. In my educational setting, the importance of rapport spans the whole school community from our faculty to students to parents.

I believe that genuine rapport is developed when people are intentional about building positive relationships. During my time in leadership, I have helped change and adapt organisational structures that have facilitated the development of rapport between my staff. Creating an environment for rapport to flourish is an essential element of leadership and often small changes to daily routines can make a big difference. Whether it is overhauling your staff meeting format or being intentional about developing effective teams, all leaders should reflect on whether they are creating an environment for relationships to develop, or if what they are doing is stifling rapport.

Neil White
Early & Primary Years Principal
GEMS World Academy
Singapore

Chapter Eleven

Your Action Plan

"Words may inspire but only action creates change."
Simon Sinek

There are many wonderful self-help books that can be read in order to improve one's self personally or professionally. However, I have found that if people don't commit to *actioning* their newfound knowledge it quickly dissipates and will rarely be implemented. The same can be said for professional development conferences or training sessions. People leave the events pumped up and ready to change their organisations, but if they do not implement something of what they have learnt within two days, there is a very small chance that it will ever be implemented. Have you ever left a training session, workshop or conference buzzing with excitement and ideas, only to fail to implement any of them? Or perhaps you have read an inspiring book, but due to the busyness of life your intended goals from the book have not been realised. I don't want this to be the case after you've read this book. The goal is action!

My intention in this final chapter is to help you formulate an action plan, with very specific goals, and then to have you begin to implement what you have learnt. I am extremely confident that the rapport-building strategies covered in this book will help you to genuinely connect with other people. Hopefully you have already attempted the exercises we talked about, which were designed to bring you an awareness of your ability within each strategy. Remember, regardless of how effective you think you are at building rapport, we can always grow and develop further strategies to help us connect more authentically. Rapport is not a destination; it is a journey that requires regular attention, commitment and intent.

If you have reflected on your interpersonal interactions and understand the importance of rapport while reading this book, I have achieved my goal. I have seen the power of rapport at work in my life both personally and professionally, and I am convinced more than ever that the ability to authentically connect with others is one of the most important life skills a person can develop. As you continue on this journey and work on the strategies mentioned in this book, you will experience a new level of connection with people. These new connections will not only encourage and energise others, but they will profoundly influence the way you view people and your daily interactions.

Before we begin our action plan, let's refocus on the WHY. Why is rapport so important that you should formulate an action plan in order to build authentic connections? I have summarised why rapport is so important in a few bullet points to help refresh your memory. Keep in mind, the benefits of rapport are extensive and will influence every area of your life, but here are three immediate outcomes.

Rapport is important because it...

- increases personal and organisational productivity
- increases collaboration and employee engagement
- builds trust between people

Action Plan

There are three parts to this action plan:

1. Firstly, you are going to create a plan on paper. While plans made in our head are wonderful, they seldom lead to success and aren't often sustainable. Writing down your action plan is proven to be way more effective. This will include an

evaluation of your organisation or work context, as well as character assessments of those you interact with daily.

2. Secondly, you will implement your action plan. Starting small, with minor adjustments to your behaviour and interactions, you will begin to focus on building rapport through every interaction you have. By raising awareness of the impact your interactions and communication have on people, you will gain further insight into your ability to build rapport.

3. Thirdly, and very importantly, you will reflect on your action plan and implementation process and then make adjustments accordingly. The process of building rapport is cyclical. It is an ongoing journey that builds upon itself. One never arrives at the finish line claiming one has all the answers. Humans are constantly evolving and experiencing different things; therefore the process of building rapport should continually evolve and be contextualised to each situation. Regular reflection throughout this process is critical.

My goal for you during the action plan process is that you gain an awareness of your ability to build rapport with people and then, using the strategies outlined in this book, begin to develop deeper and more authentic connections with those around you. I have seen these strategies work, not only in my own life, but in the lives of people around the world who believe in the power of rapport.

Action Plan - Step One

Organisational Assessment

In the space below describe your current workplace culture in five words. Take some time to reflect on the corporate culture of your organisation. Use your cognitive skills as well as your intuition to help guide you as you reflect on your workplace. Think about not only what your brain is telling you about your organisation, but also what your intuition is telling you. Write down the five words that best describe your workplace culture.

[ ]

With your workplace description in place, write down three things that you can do every day to positively impact the corporate culture of your workplace. These three actions need to be implemented daily and should be aimed at creating a positive and appreciative environment among all stakeholders. Write these three actions here.

[ ]

Now you have your first action on your action plan. While your focus is to authentically connect with individuals in your organisation, it is important to keep some attention on the corporate culture as well. Corporate culture is a litmus test for the human connections within the organisation. Poor or negative corporate culture more often than not reflects poor human connections in the company; in other words, low levels of rapport or artificial connections. Conversely, an organisation with a positive corporate culture will be built upon a foundation of rapport, appreciation and authentic connections.

Regardless of the size of your workplace, you can have an impact. Be intentional about implementing your three actions daily.

Action Plan - Step Two

Character Assessment

In this section you are going to come up with an action plan to impact five people you interact with daily. Feel free to create an action plan with more than five people, but it is probably advisable to start with a low number and then build from there. Choose five people you currently do not have a good rapport with. You may get on well with each other superficially, but there is no deep connection or emotional understanding.

Once you have selected the person, write their name down and then answer the questions about them. The questions are designed to help you reflect on the strategies outlined earlier. Then commit to consistent daily action. Remember, building rapport is more about the small things you do every day, rather than the large once-off events. Don't overthink this process; trust your intuition as well as your cognitive reasoning to come up with daily actions you can implement.

Person's Name:

Describe this person in five words:

What three strategies from the book can you use to build a connection with this person?

What three things will you do every day to build rapport with this person?

Person's Name:

Describe this person in five words:

What three strategies from the book can you use to build a connection with this person?

What three things will you do every day to build rapport with this person?

Person's Name:

Describe this person in five words:

What three strategies from the book can you use to build a connection with this person?

What three things will you do every day to build rapport with this person?

Person's Name:

Describe this person in five words:

What three strategies from this book can you use to build a connection with this person?

What three things will you do every day to build rapport with this person?

Person's Name:

Describe this person in five words:

What three strategies from this book can you use to build a connection with this person?

What three things will you do every day to build rapport with this person?

Action Plan - Step Three

Implementation

Well done! You have completed the assessment of your organisation and created a strategy to build rapport with five people within your workplace. This is a fantastic start and as I've said before, it is vital that you put into practice what you have learnt.

It is also very important that you enjoy the process of implementation. While this may be pushing you beyond your comfort zone, one does need to be extended in order to see growth. Do not fear failure or a negative outcome from your efforts. By reaching out positively and seeking to develop rapport with others, you will have an impact. Most important of all, be authentic in everything you do.

The process of implementation should initially last three to four weeks. This timeframe, if worked on consistently, will allow sufficient time for a reduction of uncertainty within the minds of the other people and the development of basic rapport. Over time, and through consistent implementation, the initial connection will become deeper and more authentic. As your connection deepens you will experience a greater connection, which can lead to more authentic collaboration, engagement and support. As you gain traction in building rapport you will see that it is an ongoing process that deepens over time.

I encourage you during this process of implementation to keep referring to the strategies outlined in this book. They are simple yet proven, and provide you with a clear outline for success.

Action Plan - Step Four

Reflection

The fourth and final step in your action plan is the process of reflection. In today's world we seldom find time to reflect on our actions, dreams and relationships, and this results in us limiting our potential to be creative and innovative. Taking time to reflect is an essential tool for success, not only in rapport-building, but in every area of our lives.

When you genuinely reflect on something, you free your mind to think critically and creatively, allowing yourself the ability to change and progress. However, if you fail to set time aside to reflect, you will never unlock your brain's powerful ability to problem-solve and evolve your thinking and worldview. You will be bound to your current thought patterns. It is only through the process of reflection that you can gain this awareness, and it is only once you have gained awareness that you can begin to regulate and change your actions.

Reflection should not only happen at the end of an event or activity. We should be constantly reflecting on our actions, interactions and abilities in order to keep developing. Our brains have an amazing ability to innovate. However, it requires time to process thoughts and emotions. Incorporating reflection into your daily habits will allow your brain this essential time to process and innovate.

There are many forms of reflection, but the commonalities between all of them is the ability to think without distraction. Some people reflect while in a state of prayer, others find reflection time by simply sitting quietly, while some find it in nature. Reflection is all about allowing your brain time to think and process the action or interaction you want to change or develop. It is important that you find a solution that is a fit for you, something that will be sustainable and relevant to your daily habits. I find that even taking a few minutes out during my day can be a great time to gather my thoughts and reflect. Although there might be chaos around me, focusing on what I am reflecting on separates me from my immediate environment.

Reflection can also be done in a group setting. By aligning thoughts on a specific topic, a group of people can reflect on something together, and often hearing one another's perspectives can drive the reflection deeper. This form of reflection is especially powerful in a classroom setting in a school or university. The sense of group discovery, where dependency is placed on each member of the group, can yield powerful insights.

For the purposes of this action plan you will be reflecting at the end of an implementation process, but reflection is most effective when done continuously, in a cyclical manner. The understanding that everything we do should migrate through a cycle of reflection is an important concept to grasp and will lead to highly effective reflection and a more integrated, authentic lifestyle.

Reflection, like many other skills, is developed through application. The more you reflect, the more attuned your brain will become to this process, and the greater the results will be. Reflection also allows you time to hear your intuition and connect your emotions to your thoughts.

As you reflect on your action plan, I would like you to focus on three questions:

1. What worked well in achieving my objective?
2. What didn't work?
3. What new strategies can I use next?

These simple questions are designed to help you bring your thoughts to the forefront of your mind. Once you have written your answers in the space provided below, reflect on these thoughts for a while and allow your brain time to process your thinking and bring new thoughts into your understanding. I encourage you to write the thoughts that come to your mind down, and then act upon them. This is the power of reflection.

What worked well in achieving my objective?

What didn't work well?

What new strategies can I use next?

Chapter Twelve

Three Final Thoughts

"There is no greater investment on earth, than the investment into another human being through daily positive interactions." Mike Gilmour

Through reading this book I truly hope that you have gained an understanding of the power of rapport, and that you are more convinced than before of the impact your interactions have on those around you. While I'm sure your interest in human interactions drew you to reading this book, I certainly hope that you are inspired to continue to build your rapport-building skills in the future. As a person fully grasps the influence relationships have on all areas of human productivity and life, a greater emphasis is placed on honing the skills required to form authentic connections. I definitely hope that you will continue to implement what you have learnt through this book in your everyday interactions. I am beyond confident that by focusing on building rapport in all areas of your life you will achieve success and accomplish great things, regardless of your context. So, in conclusion I would like to focus on three important takeaways that for me summarise *The Power of Rapport*.

1. Relationships Matter

I am regularly encouraged when I go onto my social media platforms or attend business and leadership networks and hear people speaking about the importance of relationships in the workplace. While I still believe we have a long way to go until the majority of people in the workplace truly understand the influence of positive relationships and rapport, it is encouraging to participate in the conversations that are happening. However, we know that for rapport to be built it requires more than simply an understanding that relationships matter, but rather it requires the skills to build upon this understanding.

I encourage you to find like-minded people who value relationships and rapport and begin a conversation as to what this looks like in your context, and why they are so important to you. As you begin to share your understanding and experience with others you encourage people in their interactions, but also give them practical tips to develop their skills. We are all learners on this journey and the experiences you have are valuable to others. Finding someone or a group of people you can speak to in person is always best. However, I have found that some of my best conversations around the importance of relationships and rapport have come about online through social media, Twitter and LinkedIn in particular. I have had and continue to have great discussions with like-minded educators, leaders, entrepreneurs and employees from all corners of the globe on these platforms, and every time I leave these conversations more inspired and motivated about the importance of relationships. If you are looking to get connected please do reach out to me and I'd be happy to include you in our discussions. My Twitter handle is @gilmour_mike otherwise get in touch through our website www.thepowerofrapport.com

Remember that rapport is reciprocal and will motivate, encourage and inspire you as much as it will the other person. While your intention in building rapport must never be for personal gain, you will naturally become a benefactor once in a positive relationship. Authenticity is critical in this process though and I have experienced that when you authentically reach out to build rapport with the best interests of the other person in mind, you receive so much more. It can almost be described as gaining interest on an investment. You are putting something of yours of value into another person and you receive interest on this investment. The last time I checked my investments, both myself and my broker were happy! Everyone wins when you are intentional about building authentic connections.

So as you wrap up this book I really do want you to take away the understanding that relationships matter. I believe without a doubt that rapport will increase productivity and employee longevity within your organisation. However, and equally as important, relationships and rapport will build a deeper connection and understanding with people, and the benefits of these positive connections will lead to a shared success. As you place a high level of value on the relationships and interactions you have on a daily basis, you will then begin to see your actions align with your understanding. However, the opposite is equally as true, without the understanding that relationships are valuable, your actions towards others will reflect a decreased value.

2. Action is Essential

The second takeaway I'd like to leave with you is that action is essential. While having the intention to build authentic connections is admirable, it means absolutely nothing unless you are willing to act upon those intentions. We know all relationships and human interactions require action and intentionality in order to develop. As you have experienced through this book, there are essential skills that a person needs to develop in order to become effective in building rapport. However, the intentionality to actively develop these skills ultimately separates those who will be successful from those who won't.

So I encourage you to implement the strategies and skills you have learnt about in this book every day of your life. As you allow the topic of rapport to remain in the forefront of your daily focus, you will notice an increase in both your voluntary and involuntary actions aligning with your intentions.

So, regardless of how good your rapport-building intentions are, without action they mean nothing. Your actions are essential and need to be consistent, regular and intentional.

3. Every Interaction Counts

Thirdly, and finally, I'd like to draw your focus to what probably is the most important take-away from this book. I suppose if you had to summarise this book into one paragraph it might be this one. I don't say that to downplay what has been said previously as there is tremendous value in the preceding chapters. But, I believe that every interaction a person has is valuable and either builds a person up, or brings them down. Ultimately, everything you've read about in this book can only be implemented within a human interaction. So without interactions, there is no rapport.

Earlier in the book you read about emotional reserves and how your influence on a person will either fill their emotional energy tank, or drain it. Well, this is why I place such a high emphasis on every interaction I have with people, as I know that in order to build rapport I need to be an energy-builder and not an energy-taker. When you keep this understanding in your daily focus your interactions are not solely focused on the content of the interaction. They are also focused on the manner in which you interact and how your actions influence the connection you have with the other person.

Every interaction you have is a rapport-building opportunity and needs to be viewed this way. I can guarantee that when you have this understanding your interactions will be a lot more intentional and productive. I hope that this book has inspired you to view your interactions differently so that you will see every interaction you have from now onwards as more than a simple transactional occurrence.

Relationships matter, action is essential and every interaction counts. This is the power of rapport.

Acknowledgements

There are many people who have contributed to my life and the success of this book. While the journey hasn't always been easy, I would like to express my gratitude to them here as without them this book would not have been possible. Firstly, to my wife Sandi and my two children, Maddi and Jack, who without their love, support and encouragement this book would not have happened. I am so grateful for the unique family I have and for the journey we are on in life. To my parents, brother and extended family, who shaped me into the person I am today, I am forever grateful for the opportunities you gave me and the never ending love and support you have displayed. To the contributor's in this book who invested their time and knowledge through sharing their professional perspectives on rapport. Your contributions validate the importance of rapport and I appreciate the willingness you all demonstrated in contributing to *The Power of Rapport*. To my colleagues, both past and present, thank you for teaching me so much about rapport. I appreciate the trust many of you have shown in me, and I am a better leader and person because of the opportunities I have been given. Finally, thank you to Linda and Marc for your editing work and honest feedback during the writing process.

Printed in Great Britain
by Amazon